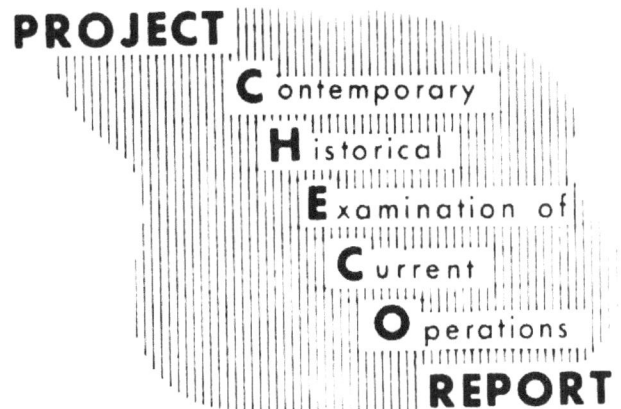

PROJECT REPORT
Contemporary **H**istorical **E**xamination of **C**urrent **O**perations

LAM SON 719 30 JANUARY - 24 MARCH 1971
THE SOUTH VIETNAMESE INCURSION INTO LAOS

24 MARCH 1971

HQ PACAF

Directorate of Operations Analysis

CHECO/CORONA HARVEST DIVISON

Prepared by:
COL J.F.LOYE, Jr
MAJ G.K.StCLAIR
MAJ L.J.JOHNSON
MR J.W. DENNISON
Project CHECO 7th AF, DOAC

PROJECT CHECO REPORTS

The counterinsurgency and unconventional warfare environment of Southeast Asia has resulted in the employment of USAF airpower to meet a multitude of requirements. The varied applications of airpower have involved the full spectrum of USAF aerospace vehicles, support equipment, and manpower. As a result, there has been an accumulation of operational data and experiences that, as a priority, must be collected, documented, and analyzed as to current and future impact upon USAF policies, concepts, and doctrine.

Fortunately, the value of collecting and documenting our SEA experiences was recognized at an early date. In 1962, Hq USAF directed CINCPACAF to establish an activity that would be primarily responsive to Air Staff requirements and direction, and would provide timely and analytical studies of USAF combat operations in SEA.

Project CHECO, an acronym for Contemporary Historical Examination of Current Operations, was established to meet this Air Staff requirement. Managed by Hq PACAF, with elements at Hq 7AF and 7AF/13AF, Project CHECO provides a scholarly, "on-going" historical examination, documentation, and reporting on USAF policies, concepts, and doctrine in PACOM. This CHECO report is part of the overall documentation and examination which is being accomplished. Along with the other CHECO publications, this is an authentic source for an assessment of the effectiveness of USAF airpower in PACOM.

ROLAND M. CAMPBELL, Major General, USAF
Chief of Staff

REPLY TO
ATTN OF: DOAD 24 March 1971

SUBJECT: Project CHECO Report, "Lam Son 719, 30 January - 24 March 1971, The South Vietnamese Incursion into Laos" (U)

SEE DISTRIBUTION PAGE

1. Attached is a SECRET NOFORN document. It shall be transported, stored, safeguarded, and accounted for in accordance with applicable security directives. SPECIAL HANDLING REQUIRED, NOT RELEASABLE TO FOREIGN NATIONALS. The information contained in this document will not be disclosed to foreign nations or their representatives. Retain or destroy in accordance with AFR 205-1. Do not return.

2. This letter does not contain classified information and may be declassified if attachment is removed from it.

FOR THE COMMANDER IN CHIEF

MAURICE L. GRIFFITH, Colonel, USAF
Chief, CHECO/CORONA HARVEST Division
Directorate of Operations Analysis
DCS/Operations

1 Atch
Proj CHECO Rprt (S/NF), 24 Mar 71

DISTRIBUTION LIST

1. SECRETARY OF THE AIR FORCE

    a. SAFAA 1
    b. SAFLL 1
    c. SAFOI 2
    d. SAFUS 1

2. HEADQUARTERS USAF

    a. AFNB. 1

    b. AFCCS
        (1) AFCCSSA 1
        (2) AFCVC 1
        (3) AFCAV 1
        (4) AFCHO 2

    c. AFCSA
        (1) AFCSAG 1
        (2) AFCSAMI 1

    d. AFOA. 1

    e. AFIGO
        (1) OSIIAP. 3
        (2) IGS 1

    f. AFSG. 1

    g. AFNIATC 5

    h. AFAAC 1
        (1) AFACMI. 1

    i. AFODC
        (1) AFPRC 1
        (2) AFPRE 1
        (3) AFPRM 1

    j. AFPDC
        (1) AFDPW. 1

    k. AFRD
        (1) AFRDP. 1
        (2) AFRDQ. 1
        (3) AFRDQPC. 1
        (4) AFRDR. 1
        (5) AFRDQL 1

    l. AFSDC
        (1) AFSLP. 1
        (2) AFSME. 1
        (3) AFSMS. 1
        (4) AFSSS. 1
        (5) AFSTP. 1

    m. AFTAC. 1

    n. AFXO 1
        (1) AFXOB. 1
        (2) AFXOD. 1
        (3) AFXODC 1
        (4) AFXODD 1
        (5) AFXODL 1
        (6) AFXOOAB. 1
        (7) AFXOSL 1
        (8) AFXOOSN. 1
        (9) AFXOOSO. 1
       (10) AFXOOSS. 1
       (11) AFXOOSV. 1
       (12) AFXOOTR. 1
       (13) AFXOOTW. 1
       (14) AFXOOTZ. 1
       (15) AFXOOCY. 1
       (16) AF/XOX 6
       (17) AFXOXXG. 1

3. MAJOR COMMAND

   a. TAC

      (1) HEADQUARTERS
         (a) DO. 1
         (b) XP. 2
         (c) DOCC. 1
         (d) DREA. 1
         (e) IN. 1

      (2) AIR FORCES
         (a) 12AF
             1. DOO. 1
             2. IN 1
         (b) 19AF(IN). 1
         (c) USAFSOF(DO) 1

      (3) WINGS
         (a) 1SOW(DOI) 1
         (b) 23TFW(DOI). 1
         (c) 27TRW(DOI). 1
         (d) 33TFW(DOI). 1
         (e) 64TAW(DOI). 1
         (f) 67TRW(DOI). 1
         (g) 75TRW(DOI). 1
         (h) 316TAW(DOX) 1
         (i) 317TAW(DOI) 1
         (j) 363TRW(DOI) 1
         (k) 464TFW(DOI) 1
         (l) 474TFW(DOI) 1
         (m) 479TFW(DOI) 1
         (n) 516TAW(DOX) 1
         (o) 4403TFW(DOI). 1
         (p) 58TAC FTR TNG WG. . 1
         (q) 354TFW(DOI) 1
         (r) 60MAWg(DOOXI) . . . 1

      (4) TAC CENTERS, SCHOOLS
         (a) USAFTAWC(DRA) . . . 1
         (b) USAFTFWC(DRA) . . . 1
         (c) USAFAGOS(EDA) . . . 1

   b. SAC

      (1) HEADQUARTERS
         (a) DOPL. 1
         (b) XPX 1
         (c) DM. 1
         (d) IN. 1
         (e) OA. 1
         (f) HO. 1

      (2) AIR FORCES
         (a) 2AF(INCS) 1
         (b) 8AF(DOA). 2
         (c) 15AF(INCE). 1

   c. MAC

      (1) HEADQUARTERS
         (a) DOI 1
         (b) DOO 1
         (c) CSEH. 1
         (d) MACOA 1

      (2) MAC SERVICES
         (a) AWS(HO) 1
         (b) ARRS(XP). 1
         (c) ACGS(CGO) 1

   d. ADC

      (1) HEADQUARTERS
         (a) DO. 1
         (b) DOT 1
         (c) XPC 1

(2) AIR DIVISIONS
    (a) 25AD(DOI) 1
    (b) 29AD(DO). 1
    (c) 20AD(DOI) 1

e. ATC
  (1) DOSPI 1

f. AFLC
  (1) HEADQUARTERS
    (a) XOX 1

g. AFSC
  (1) HEADQUARTERS
    (a) XRP 1
    (b) XRLW. 1
    (c) SAMSO(XRW). 1
    (d) SDA 1
    (e) CSH 2
    (f) DLXP. 1
    (g) ASD(RWST) 1
    (h) ESD(XO) 1
    (i) RADC(DOTL). 1
    (j) ADTC(CCS) 1
    (k) ADTC(SSLT). 1
    (l) ESD(YW) 1
    (m) AFATL(DL) 1

h. USAFSS
  (1) HEADQUARTERS
    (a) AFSCC(SUR). 1

  (2) SUBORDINATE UNITS
    (a) Eur Scty Rgn(OPD-P) . 1
    (b) 6940 Scty Wg (OOD). . 1

i. AAC
  (1) HEADQUARTERS
    (a) ALDOC-A 1

j. USAFSO
  (1) HEADQUARTERS
    (a) CSH. 1

k. PACAF
  (1) HEADQUARTERS
    (a) DP 1
    (b) IN 1
    (c) XP 2
    (d) CSH. 1
    (e) DOAD 5
    (f) DC 1
    (g) DM 1

  (2) AIR FORCES
    (a) 5AF
      1. CSH 1
      2. XP. 1
      3. DO. 1
    (b) Det 8, ASD(DOASD). . 1
    (c) 7AF
      1. DO. 1
      2. IN. 1
      3. XP. 1
      4. DOCT. 1
      5. DOAC. 2
    (d) 13AF
      1. CSH 1
      2. XP. 1
    (e) 7/13AF(CHECO). . . . 1

  (3) AIR DIVISIONS
    (a) 313AD(DOI) 1
    (b) 314AD(XOP) 2
    (c) 327AD
      1. IN. 1
    (d) 834AD(DO). 2

(4) WINGS
    (a) 8TFW(DOEA) 1
    (b) 12TFW(DOIN) 1
    (c) 35TFW(DOIN) 1
    (d) 56SOW(WHD) 1
    (e) 366TFW(DO) 1
    (f) 388TFW(DO) 1
    (g) 405TFW(DOEA) 1
    (h) 432TRW(DOI) 1
    (i) 460TRW(DOI) 1
    (j) 475TFW(DCO) 1
    (k) 1st Test Sq(A) 1

(5) OTHER UNITS
    (a) Task Force ALPHA(IN) . . 1
    (b) 504TASG(DO) 1
    (c) Air Force Advisory Gp. . 1

1. USAFE

   (1) HEADQUARTERS
      (a) DOA 1
      (b) DOLO 1
      (c) DOO 1
      (d) XDC 1

   (2) AIR FORCES
      (a) 3AF(DO) 2
      (b) 16AF(DO) 1
      (c) 17AF(IN) 1

   (3) WINGS
      (a) 36TFW(DCOID) 1
      (b) 50TFW(DOA) 1
      (c) 20TFW(DOI) 1
      (d) 81TRW(DCOI) 1
      (e) 401TFW(DCOI) 1
      (f) 513TAW(DOI) 1

4. SEPARATE OPERATING AGENCIES
   a. ACIC(DOP) 2
   b. AFRES(XP) 2
   c. AU
      1. ACSC(SA 1
      2. AUL(SE)-69-108 2
      3. ASI(ASD-1) 1
      4. ASI(HOA) 2
   d. ANALYTIC SERVICES, INC . 1
   e. USAFA
      1. DFH 1

TABLE OF CONTENTS

	Page
FOREWORD	xii
CHAPTER I - OVERVIEW	1
COMMAND AND CONTROL	11
AIR SUPPORT OF LAM SON 719	13
INTERIM ASSESSMENT OF AIR SUPPORT FOR LAM SON 719	16
INTERDICTION	17
SUPPRESSION OF AA FIRE	18
USE OF TAC AIR AGAINST ENEMY ARMOR	19
AIR SUPPORT IN LANDING ZONE PREPARATION	20
CHAPTER II - PLANNING FOR LAM SON 719	22
CONCEPT OF OPERATIONS	22
THE PLANNED PHASES	22
Phase I	23
Phase II	24
Phase III	25
Phase IV	25
A COMBINED OPERATION	26
CONTROL OF TACTICAL AIR	28
FORCES COMMITTED	32
Friendly Air	32
Friendly Ground Forces	33
Enemy Forces	34
CHAPTER III - THE CAMPAIGN	35
DEPLOYMENT OF U.S. FORCES	35
AIRLIFT EFFORT	36
ARVN ASSEMBLY	40
JUMP-OFF	40
DRIVE TO A LOUI	42
CONSOLIDATION	45
SEARCHING FOR CACHES	46
ENEMY TROOP DISPOSITION	48
SCREENING TECHNIQUES OF U.S. FORCES	50
ARVN TACTICS	50
RANGER HILL	51
LULL IN THE FIGHTING	52
LOGISTICAL SUPPORT AT KHE SANH	53
ARC LIGHT	54

	Page
TACTICAL AIR	56
ENEMY STRIKES HARD - OBJECTIVE 31	56
RAID TO TCHEPONE	62
LZ LO LO	62
LZ LIZ	63
MARINES REPLACE THE 1ST INFANTRY	63
LZ SOPHIA	63
LZ HOPE	64
SEARCH AND DESTROY	64
HIGH WATER MARK - TCHEPONE	65
ENEMY BUILD-UP	66
RETURN TO THE EAST	67
WITHDRAWAL FROM LAOS	68
LO LO ABANDONED	69
THE RAIDERS ARE BLOODIED	70
HASTENED WITHDRAWAL	72
EVACUATION FROM A LOUI	72
ALL UNITS IN CONTACT	73
ARMOR IN TROUBLE	74
ALL OUT BUT THE STRAGGLERS	76
LAM SON EAST	78
CHAPTER IV - AIR SUPPORT IN LAM SON 719	80
PLANNING AIR SUPPORT	80
Sortie Allocations	80
Security Aspects	82
PROBLEMS ARISING FROM VIETNAMESE CONTROL	82
Command Structure	82
Language Problems	84
TACTICAL AIR CONTROL	85
AIRMOBILE OPERATIONS	87
LANDING ZONE PREPARATIONS	90
LZ Lo Lo	93
Summary	97
LZ Liz	97
LZ Sophia	99
LZ Hope	100
RESUPPLY AND EXTRACTION	101
CLOSE AIR SUPPORT	103
ATTACKS AGAINST AIR DEFENSES	108
Defenses Against Fixed Wing Aircraft	109
Defenses Against Helicopters	110
Weapons Employed Against Defenses	110

		Page
	ATTACKS AGAINST ARMOR	112
	INTERDICTION	116
	ARC LIGHT	117
	SHORT ROUNDS	120
	AIRCRAFT LOSSES	121
	IMPLICATIONS FOR FUTURE OPERATIONS	122

EPILOGUE 126

SCENARIO 127

APPENDIX

   A. STATISTICAL APPENDIX 131
   B. LOGISTICS MOVEMENT APPENDIX 141

FOOTNOTES

   Foreword 151
   Chapter I 151
   Chapter II 153
   Chapter III 154
   Chapter IV 160

GLOSSARY 163

RESEARCH NOTE 166

FIGURES   Follows Page

  1. (S) Lam Son 719 4
  2. (S) Sensor Detected Truck Movements in Lam Son Area 18
  3. (C) Three Destroyed Tanks 20
  4. (C) Bomb Damage Assessment/Overrun of ARVN Strong Points 20
  5. (S) Base Areas 26
  6. (S) Lam Son 719 Control Centers 30
  7. (U) First C-130 to Land at Khe Sanh 38
  8. (C) ARVN Fire Support Base 38
  9. (S) Order of Battle - 12 Feb 71 50
10. (C) Overrun Fire Support Base on Hill 31 60
11. (C) Destroyed PT-76 Tank 60
12. (S) Order of Battle - 7 Mar 71 66
13. (S) U.S. Tactical Air Sorties in Steel Tiger 80

FIGURES	Follows Page
14. (S) U.S. Strike Sorties	82
15. (S) Arc Light Strikes in LZ Areas	98
16. (S) Attacks Against Enemy Tanks	114
17. (S) Aircraft Combat Losses in Lam Son 719	122
18. (S) Location Fixed Wing Combat Losses	122

FOREWORD

This CHECO report on Lam Son 719, the South Vietnamese incursion into Laos in February and March 1971, is an interim narrative of what was one of the most significant military actions in Southeast Asia since the enemy's 1968 Tet Offensive. It also is a report on one of the most fundamental problems faced by Americans in the Vietnam conflict--the proper employment of American technological superiority, mainly air power, against an enemy highly skilled in the elusive art of jungle warfare and equipped with modern sophisticated weaponry with the exception of aircraft. Lam Son 719 was the first major operation of its kind - a cross-border activity in which large South Vietnamese ground forces operated independently without U.S. Army ground advisors but with almost complete dependence upon U.S. air support. Yet in Lam Son 719, some of the problems associated with the U.S. effort since 1962 reappeared and had to be resolved to meet the particular situation. Primary among these was the before-the-fact coordination of air support for ground or airmobile operations to fit the needs of a fluid ground situation. Also of significance was the problem of locating the enemy and bringing the maximum firepower to bear on him. Despite these problems, Lam Son 719 showed that a large Vietnamese ground force, which had remained on the sidelines for years, could move into the enemy stronghold given U.S. air support. This was a critical test of its capability, a test which would have a great impact upon plans for American withdrawal from Vietnam.

The history of air power in Vietnam is replete with examples of problems concerning the proper application of air technology, problems which reappeared in Lam Son 719. A brief review of some of these experiences may be valuable in putting the Lam Son 719 report in perspective. As early as December 1964 at Binh Gia, 40 miles east of Saigon, the first enemy-division-sized attack of the war took place, launching what General Giap considered the beginning of the final phase of the war.[1/] In this battle, where a Vietnamese Marine Battalion and Ranger Battalion were practically wiped out, tactical air was not called in during the critical phase of the fighting and the heliborne firepower which was used was ineffective against an enemy operating under heavy foliage. As a result of this action, General Westmoreland had his staff reappraise the role of tactical air in the fighting.[2/] In October 1965, the 1st Air Cavalry Division in its first major engagement in Vietnam in the battle of the Ia Drang Valley, suffered some 250 men killed, most during a single ambush in which tactical air was not used to full effect. The 1st Air Cavalry Division, in this battle, was determined to use its organic helicopters for supply and suppressive fire and called on the U.S. Air Force only after its helicopter in-commission rate dropped to an intolerable low.[3/] The question of the number of tactical air sorties required in support of ground operations became a major issue during Operation Birmingham in early 1966. For this one ground operation, the U.S. Army commander requested on one day 284 sorties, which was then 63% of the total available throughout Vietnam. In this case, the USAF protested the inordinate call upon air resources and COMUSMACV directed a more realistic tasking of tactical air.[4/] A major breakthrough in proper coordination and control of the theater air capability came in early 1968 when the Deputy COMUSMACV for Air was made single manager for all USAF and U.S. Marine air resources in Vietnam but only after serious air coordination problems were experienced in major campaigns in the DMZ area of Vietnam.[5/]

These were only a few examples of many battles and campaigns fought over six years which guided to a large extent the evolution of air tactics, command and control, and general strategy concerning the use of air power. At Lam Son 719, this past experience was put to a major test.

Not since the Ia Drang Valley battle of November 1965 when the Army's new 1st Air Cavalry Division was engaged in its first battle has hard information on an operation in Southeast Asia been so difficult for the AF to obtain, as it was in Lam Son 719 in February-March 1971. In both battles, there was reason to question the accuracy of some statistics concerning losses of personnel and equipment, particularly helicopters. But in Lam Son 719, the problem was compounded by the fact that the Vietnamese were fighting in Laos without their U.S. advisors and there was no way to confirm their reports. There were highly conflicting statistics generated by Lam Son 719, some due to duplication of BDA reports and some to reporting problems. For this reason and because this report was completed shortly after the end of the operation, the account of the operation given here can be considered only as an interim report.

To assist researchers for a later report on this highly significant operation, every available document on the subject has been placed on microfilm, including daily reports by the FACs, Hq MACV, the ABCCC and DASC Victor.

In considering air support for Lam Son 719 (tac air, helicopters, airlift and B-52s) there are several areas which are significant. First, although it has never appeared in an official report on the operation, without the air superiority provided by the U.S. Air Force over the battlefield, there could have been no Lam Son 719. Second, the tactical airlift support during the deployment, employment and subsequent resupply phases of the operation provided the critical margin of rapid troop and supply transport essential to the sustained ground combat. Third, the helilifting of friendly troops to landing zones near Tchepone would have been virtually impossible without intensive prepping by tac air and B-52s. Nor could the friendly forces, outnumbered and on unfamiliar terrain, have survived without support by tac air, gunships and B-52s. Another key fact was the effective employment of air in disrupting the enemy's plans and hindering him from massing, a particularly important issue when it is considered that the enemy had at least two months forewarning of the operation. 6/

When he did mass his forces to strike exposed and vulnerable positions, the enemy suffered heavy casualties from tac air and B-52s. Tac air was also invaluable in suppressing the fire of enemy antiaircraft (AA) weapons which included antiaircraft artillery, machine guns, small arms, mortars, rockets and grenades. While the Army did lose an estimated 200-plus helicopters destroyed plus several hundred damaged, it is awesome to imagine what the losses would have been without AA suppression. Finally, and what may historically prove to be the most important contribution of tac air to the campaign was the battle against enemy armor. The North Vietnamese had committed an estimated 120 tanks to the battle, many of them T-54s with 100mm cannons and 12.7mm machine guns and the evidence indicates that this force was ready to spring a trap on the withdrawing ARVN forces in the critical last days of the battle. That they did not is unquestionable because tac air knocked out or forced into hiding practically every tank that exposed itself in the critical 19-24 March period.

There were some weaknesses in tac air support of Lam Son 719 and these are depicted throughout this report. They include such problems as having the right ordnance at the right time and adverse weather. And there is no question that the Army aviators in their helicopters performed with the utmost courage and dedication in what was unquestionably the most difficult mission ever assigned to helicopters. That tactical air and helicopter operations each had a role to play in an operation such as Lam Son 719 was proven time and time again. FACs for example, sometimes had the choppers mark their targets so fighters could be brought in. On balance, however, the Lam Son 719 operation showed that in a "midintensity" environment, the professionalism and experience of USAF pilots, FACs and their commanders, were crucial to survival of a ground force. Perhaps the best evidence of this is the fact that only five fixed wing strike aircraft were lost in some 24,000 attacks on the enemy.

It is not the purpose of this report to emphasize the polemics of operation. This is, however, an area which must be closely examined by analysts and historians if the true impact of the role of air power in Lam Son 719 is to be determined.

CHAPTER I

OVERVIEW

Operation Lam Son 719 was a South Vietnamese three-division-sized thrust into Laos along Route 9 between Khe Sanh and Tchepone conducted between 30 January and 24 March and supported by U.S. ground and air forces. Fighting during this incursion was the heaviest of the war since the 1968 Tet Offensive. The enemy was forewarned and had positioned tanks, artillery, antiaircraft weapons and ground units in preparation for the ARVN assault, using ten to twelve regiments from five of his best divisions and an armored regiment of some 120 tanks for a total personnel force of some 35,000 combat and support troops. Unlike the fighting in Tet 1968, the Lam Son 719 campaign involved conventional warfare maneuvers by both sides using tanks and artillery against each other. The ARVN had the advantage of air support and air mobility, while the enemy had greater knowledge of the terrain, was fighting from defensive positions near his logistics base and had advance warning of the operation. There were strong indications that the enemy had made a major commitment to deal a heavy blow to ARVN forces and win a psychological victory, if not a military one.

When the Lam Son fighting ended, the South Vietnamese claimed over 13,000 enemy killed and more than 20,000 tons of weapons and ammunition captures or destroyed, much of it by air strikes. Temporary interdiction of the enemy supply routes was also claimed. Friendly casualties were high, too. Officially, ARVN casualties were listed at some 5000 killed and wounded. The U.S. lost 137 killed and had 818 wounded. Helicopter losses were officially placed at 105 destroyed and some 600 damaged, of which 20% of the latter (using the Army's yardstick) were not expected to fly again. Seven fixed wing aircraft (five strike aircraft and two others) were lost to hostile ground fire in the operation.

It is too early to determine the success or failure of Lam Son 719 or to measure its results in terms of cost effectiveness. Unquestionably, the enemy suffered heavily in men and materiel, mainly because he massed his forces to strike at the ARVN, thus creating lucrative targets for artillery and air delivered fire power. The ARVN had three of its finest divisions, the 1st Infantry, 1st Airborne and Marine Division, heavily battered before reaching its initially planned objectives. The operation should be evaluated eventually in terms of both the enemy initiative in South Vietnam and Cambodia and in terms of ARVN morale and efficiency in reaching Vietnamization goals. It is not too early as of this writing, however, to examine some of the specific problems faced in this operation, particularly those related to air support, and to evaluate them in terms of future operations.

The original Lam Son 719 plan would have placed the three-division RVNAF force along Route 9 into the Tchepone area, the supply hub of the Ho Chi Minh Trail. From positions along key enemy infiltration routes and supported by air power, it was hoped that this force would reduce the enemy logistics flow until the rains came in early May, making the roads unusable. The friendly force was also expected to sweep southwest of Tchepone down Route 914 through a major enemy storage area called Base Area 611 and back into South Vietnam through the A Shau Valley. If these goals could have been reached, enemy plans for offensive action in the northernmost Military Region I area would have been severely crimped. 7/

The plan, however, was not carried out as originally envisioned. Although the ARVN force did claim destruction of large enemy caches and the killing of more than 13,000 enemy troops, the incursion fell short of original goals. There were several reasons why. The primary one was that the enemy had positioned an unexpectedly large force along Route 9 and the key objective of Tchepone. Another reason was that enemy anti-aircraft defenses disrupted aerial mobility operations which relied heavily on vulnerable helicopters for resupply, troop movement and fire suppression. Other factors which disrupted original plans were weather, command and control problems, logistical difficulties and the serviceability of Route 9, the main incursion route. These problems are covered later in this report. Although 7th Air Force, with its seven year experience in flying the Lao Panhandle, had advised the Army of the AA threat there, the Army did not consider it a real deterrent.

There were three major decisions made during Lam Son 719 which influenced its course and chances of success. The first was on 12 February after the initial ARVN force found difficulty in reaching A Loui, the first

3

objective, due to poor road conditions and enemy harassment. President Thieu, after getting an assessment from General Lam at Quang Tri, directed that the ARVN emphasis be shifted from Tchepone to the A Loui area near the junction of Route 92 and 9 and that only a limited force go into the key enemy logistics base.[8/] Thus, instead of moving units frequently throughout the operational area and reducing their vulnerability, the main force and its flanking units in many cases assumed static positions. This was to play into the enemy's hands at a later critical stage of the operation. (See Figure 1).

The second major decision was made on 3 March after a disastrous helicopter assault into Landing Zone Lo Lo which cost the Army seven helicopters destroyed, and 42 hit and 20 declared nonflyable. Following this incident General Abrams directed that closer coordination be given to landing zone preparation. Following this direction, tactical air was brought into the Lam Son 719 operations on a much larger scale coincident with the move of additional ARVN infantry battalions into the Tchepone area landing zones. In the next three days, the three landing zones planned for the Tchepone operations - Liz, Sophia and Hope - were heavily prepped by USAF B-52s and tac air for over a period of several hours prior to the assault. The Army, after the LZ Lo Lo experience on 3 March, dropped its "go it alone" tendency.[9/]

The third and probably most critical decision of the operation came on 18 March when General Lam, his forces widely scattered and practically all under attack, was faced with the choice of sending in reinforcements

4

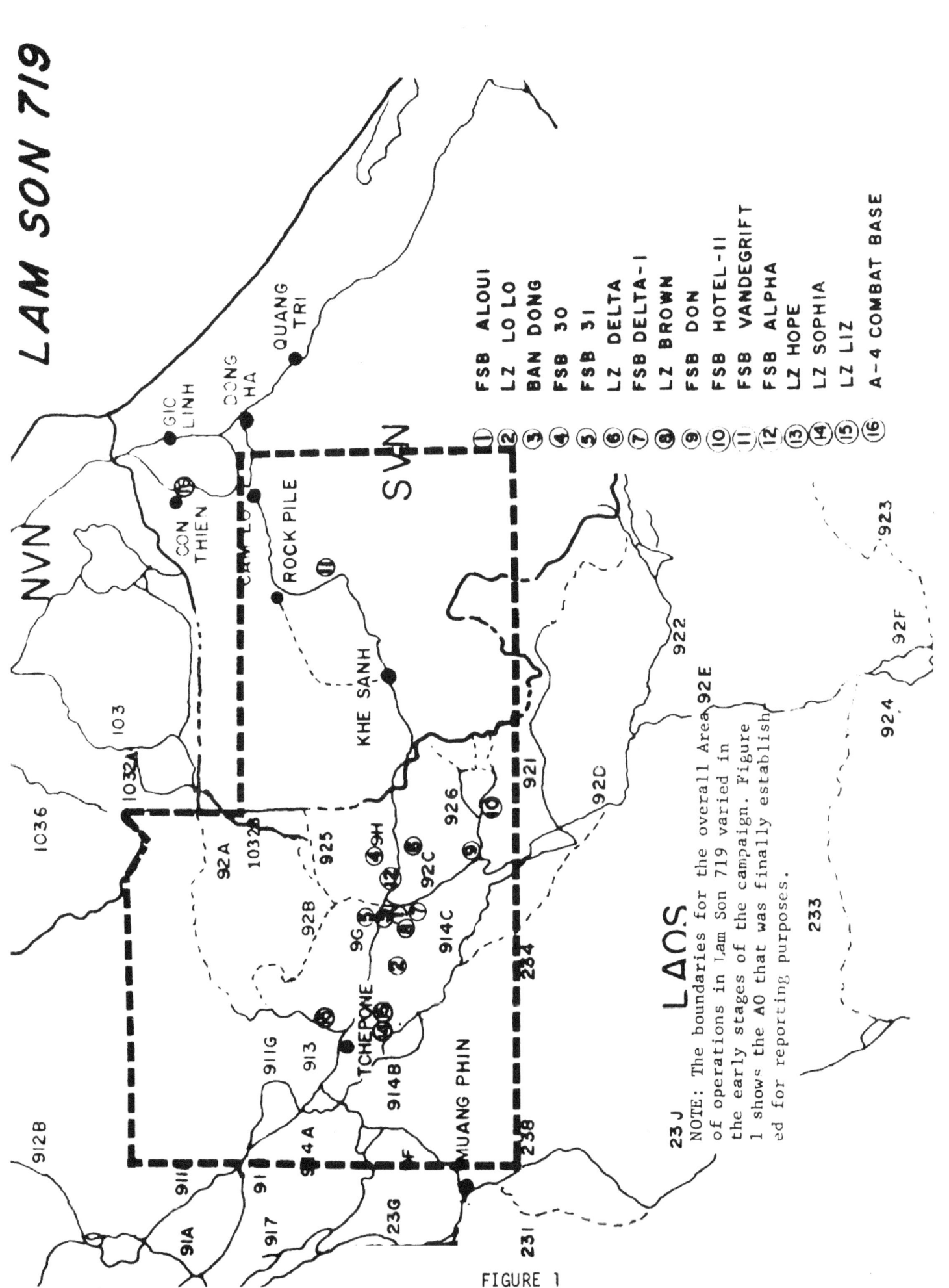

FIGURE 1

or withdrawing. He chose to withdraw despite pressure from General
Sutherland to send in reinforcements and hold in Laos. At that time,
General Lam's forces were not in a solid tactical position, with several
multibattalion units at different locations on hills south of Route 9
and on Route 9 itself.[10/] The enemy, either because of willful restraint
or because his own plans were disrupted by air attacks, had not fully
committed his forces, but beginning around 18 March practically every
ARVN unit in Laos was in contact. The general tactics of the enemy were
to hit an ARVN static location with rockets and artillery, then surround
it and move in so close to the wire with a barrage fire capability that
helicopters could not get in. Many ARVN commanders, with the enemy so
close, were reluctant to call in helicopters or tac air and walked off
the besieged sites with their casualties if possible, but too often
leaving their artillery pieces behind. Once the withdrawal began, the
enemy turned on the heat and several ARVN units were temporarily isolated.
Their commanders were not always sure where their units were, making air
support difficult. General Lam recognized that many of his positions
were becoming untenable, causing the orderly withdrawal to become a hasty
one. The ARVN forces left behind 125 tanks and armored vehicles in these
last few days but managed to get out of Laos with most of their manpower
intact.[11/]

Later chapters of this report will detail command and control aspects
of the operation and a chronology of its high points with emphasis upon
the air support provided the ARVN ground forces. However, a brief chronology

of the campaign, emphasizing the critical last days may be helpful to the reader.* Between D-Day, 30 January, and 8 February when the first ARVN units went into Laos, forces were being positioned near the Lao border and logistics routes were being opened, including the clearing of Route 9 from Dong Ha to the border and the preparation of an airstrip at Khe Sanh to receive C-130 troops and cargo flights. On 8 February, ARVN airborne battalions moved to strategic hill locations (30 and 31) some five kilometers north of the junction of Route 9 and 92 which were reached by the Armored Brigade Task Force on 10 February. Other battalions from the 1st Infantry were sent to positions south of Route 9 when the operation started. Up to this point, the operation was proceeding according to plan, but the armored column found the going slow. This, coupled with enemy resistance and the unfortunate loss of General Lam's G-3 and G-4 in a chopper crash on 9 February, prompted the change of plans by President Thieu. With the ARVN units holding fixed positions, rather than maneuvering throughout the area as originally planned, the first sign of serious trouble came on 18-20 February when the enemy struck hard at the 39th Ranger Battalion's position using artillery, mortar and human wave attacks. The Rangers were driven off the hill and suffered such heavy losses that they

---

*Data used in this chronology were extracted from a variety of sources, including COMUSMACV messages, Lam Son Daily Intelligence briefs and XXIV Corps files. Detailed references are provided in the expanded chronology of Chapter III.

were withdrawn from the campaign. But in assaulting the Rangers the enemy had massed his troops, exposing himself to the killing firepower of B-52 strikes, tactical air and gunships. The enemy dead numbered more than 600, most of them killed by air. Later, on 25-27 February, the enemy attacked airborne units on Objectives 30 and 31 using coordinated artillery, armor and massed infantry assaults.

Up to this time, U.S. Army helicopter support of the ARVN had assumed a set pattern and Army officers were confident they could provide the necessary preparation of landing zones for aerial mobility of ground forces. Light enemy opposition to early heliborne assaults added to Army confidence. For example, on 24 February, only ten tactical air strikes were used to suppress enemy antiaircraft fire around LZ Brick. The major disaster at LZ Lo Lo on 3 March changed the Army's attitude. Not only was more air used in LZ preps thereafter but the average daily USAF sortie rate for direct support of ground forces in Lam Son 719 more than double from 104 sorties per day prior to 3 March to 211 sorties in the latter part of the operation.

With the move out of Tchepone, the operation moved into a withdrawal phase which was greatly hastened by heavy enemy attacks beginning on 13 March when Lo Lo was attacked by a multiregiment enemy force, ultimately forcing its evacuation and the abandonment of eight howitzers. The enemy took the offensive, committing tanks and artillery and manpower in large numbers, and engaging every ARVN unit in Laos by the 20th of

March.

The most critical phase of the operation came between 18-24 March when the last ARVN units were extracted. A study of the daily intelligence summaries prepared by the Hammer FACs, the COMUSMACV messages to CINCPAC and other sources reveals a picture of enemy tanks emerging from positions throughout the Lam Son 719 area in Laos and moving in the direction of the main ARVN force which began withdrawing from A Loui on 19 March heading east for the RVN border along Route 9. On these last three critical days, enemy tanks were appearing in daylight moving along Routes 92 and 9. The enemy was apparently aiming at cutting off the retreating ARVN Armored Brigade and Airborne units moving overland on Route 9 and the Marine Brigade on LZ Delta, the last South Vietnamese unit to leave Laos.

The chronology of these last critical days is covered in detail in Chapter III of this report. Briefly, the ARVN armored column of 100 vehicles with its covering airborne units abandoned its base at A Loui on 19 March reaching a point on 21 March some five miles from the border. Throughout the morning and afternoon of the 21st, the column was attacked by enemy forces on both sides of the road, losing six tanks. The road was blocked and the Armored Task Force (TF) commander decided to leave Route 9 and move south to a fork in the Xe Pon River.

There were 31 separate visual sightings of enemy tanks reported between 19 and 22 March, including a report of "many enemy tanks" headed south toward A Loui on the morning of 19 March. The most significant sighting, however, came on the afternoon of 22 March when 20 enemy tanks, including T-54s, with 100mm cannons and 12.7mm machine guns in the turrets, were sighted moving at 35 miles an hour west on Route 9 just four miles behind the stalled armored task force at the Xe Pon River, obviously in an effort to catch up with the ARVN force. Other tanks were reported coming from the southwest. In what could well have been the most significant air strikes of the whole campaign, F-100s attacked part of this enemy column at 1445 on the 22d, destroying the three lead tanks. One F-100 was shot down by a tank in this attack, but the attack definitely stopped the enemy's advance and the remaining tanks dispersed. This air attack, plus other attacks elsewhere, allowed the ARVN column to cross the river to safety on 23 March, although 39 of its tanks were left behind, to be destroyed the next day by tac air after the enemy was seen manning the guns of the friendly tanks. In the next two days, enemy tanks were being reported and struck in several places throughout the Lam Son 719 area, indicating that he may have committed his armor too late. Previously the enemy's tanks were reported at various phases of the operation in caves or camouflaged off main roads, apparently to be ready for use at the right time. That these formidable weapon systems were not able to close a trap on the withdrawing forces was primarily the result of tactical air strikes, which accounted for 74 tanks destroyed and 24 damaged.[12/] Army helicopters destroyed six. If the tanks were the enemy's trump card, as events would indicate, they were overtrumped by air power. On the 22d when the enemy tanks appeared in larger strength than ever before, the enemy was in contact with every RVN unit in Laos. Simultaneously and undoubtedly in coordination with an overall plan, artillery and mortar attacks on Khe Sanh reached a peak for the operation on this day. There were four separate attacks by fire on Khe Sanh on the 22d, and 204 rounds impacted on the airfield.

While the armored column was moving for safety across the border, the 147th Marine Brigade was surrounded by enemy troops and armor on LZ Delta south of Route 9 about 15 kilometers from the border. Repeated efforts to extricate this force by helicopter failed. When the first exfiltration attempt was made on 20 March, 7th Air Force was not told about it. This lapse to the "go it alone" procedures used early in the operation proved expensive. The Army initially reported that 13 helicopters were destroyed, 50 hit and 28 rendered nonflyable, but these figures were later revised to seven destroyed and 50 hit. The fighting around Delta involved tanks as well as enemy troops and artillery. There was continuous contact, and some of the heaviest casualties of the operation resulted. In the next few days, with the 1st Infantry and most of the Airborne/Armored Task Force out of Laos, the peak number of tactical air sorties in direct support of Lam Son 719 was reached, rising to 330 on the 25th of March.

When ARVN forces crossed back into RVN, the enemy had eleven regiments and an armored regiment strung along Route 9 and north and south of the ARVN retreat route from Tchepone to the South Vietnam border. They were all on the offensive. Most of the 125 abandoned ARVN tanks and armored vehicles were left behind in these last few days. There were also reports that, in at least one extraction, ARVN troops were so desperate they clung to the skids of helicopters taking off from the pick up zone. The ARVN escaped what appeared to be a Giap-style trap carefully prepared to spring at the critical moment.

COMMAND AND CONTROL

In Lam Son 719, the ARVN ground forces under General Lam went into Laos without U.S. advisors. U.S. Army forces under the CG, XXIV Corps provided artillery, air mobility and logistical support from bases on the RVN side of the border. The tactical air, B-52 and airlift support provided from USAF, USN and USMC resources were under the direction of the Commander, 7AF. The system in Lam Son 719 was further complicated by the fact that General Lam responded to orders received directly from RVN President Nguyen Van Thieu and the two were in frequent communication making decisions on the battle plan. The significance of this relationship cannot be overemphasized, for it governed the complete course of the operation reducing U.S. control, but at the same time providing a better insight into the "Vietnamization" process. There were some problems of coordination and language which arose at times during the operation but generally, considering the situation, the command and control arrangement functioned satisfactorily. 13/

The air control system was adapted for Lam Son 719 by forming a new direct air support center next to the XXIV Corps Forward Headquarters in Quang Tri to handle air support. DASC Victor, as the control agency was called, had tactical air control parties (TACPs) at each of the three

ARVN division tactical operations centers (DTOCs). DASC Victor was practically an extension of "Blue Chip", the 7th AF Command Post at Tan Son Nhut, which also controlled the Airborne Battlefield Command and Control Centers (ABCCC) over Steel Tiger - Hillsboro or Moonbeam (effectively dedicated to Lam Son 719 during the campaign). These arrangements gave 7th AF Headquarters a direct control of tactical air support.

During the initial phase of Lam Son 719, tactical airlift support was conducted in the regular pattern, with control exercised through the 834th Air Division Airlift Control Center (ALCC) at Tan Son Nhut to the Airlift Control Elements (ALCEs) at Dong Ha, Quang Tri and Da Nang. The 834th Air Division established a forward airlift task force element at Da Nang to perform the required planning and liaison functions with the XXIV Corps staff. As the Lam Son 719 operation progressed, this task force element was expanded to include a detachment of C-130 aircraft, aircrews, operations and maintenance personnel. Subsequent to 15 February with the opening of the assault strip at Khe Sanh, the bulk of the airlift support to Lam Son 719 was provided by this Da Nang element. Based on the necessity to closely control the flow of airlift traffic into Khe Sanh, which was severely limited initially in aircraft parking capability, an artillery free air corridor was established from Hue into Khe Sanh. The Da Nang airlift element was then able to regulate the flow of aircraft into the corridor based on the ground capacity of Khe Sanh to park, off-load and relaunch the aircraft.

AIR SUPPORT OF LAM SON 719

During the period of this report, U.S. tactical air flew more than 8000 attack sorties for Lam Son 719 dropping some 20,000 tons of ordnance. These tactical air strikes were controlled by as many as six FACs operating in an area of only 550 square miles.* In addition, periodic Arc Light strikes and literally hundreds of helicopters flying from deck level to 4000 feet were also in the area. A "No Bomb Line" (NBL) was set up five miles beyond the fire support control line so that there would be a buffer zone between Lam Son 719 and air operations in the rest of Steel Tiger (Laos Panhandle). 14/ The "No Bomb Line" moved as the area of ground operations expanded and contracted.

Various types of ordnance were used to handle a variety of ground situations, but the majority of fighters carried high-drag bombs and napalm, a mix proven very effective for close support. At least one flight an hour carried CBU or some special-purpose ordnance such as Rockeye for use against armor. For LZ preps, C-130s dropped "Commando Vault" 15,000 pound BLU-82 bombs with extended fuses. 15/

Targeting for tactical air had to be flexible in that only half the RVNAF requests were for hard targets. The DASC Victor director arranged

---

*There was also an additional roaming FAC who flew on the northern and western perimeters of the AO to serve as an artillery spotter and to reconnoiter enemy troop movements in the area.

with the Army to provide him with a "bank" of targets that the FAC could keep in his "hip pocket" and use when air could not go elsewhere. Troops in contact (TIC) had the highest priority for sorties with other immediates such as attacks on enemy armor also getting top attention. There were times, particularly during the withdrawal period, when there were several TICs at one time, making it difficult to respond immediately to all of them. 16/

From 8 February to 24 March, B-52s flew 1358 sorties and dropped more than 32,000 tons of bombs. These strikes were made around the clock. The drops in some cases were made closer to friendly troops than ever before (some within 300 yards). The B-52s were capable of a faster response to hot targets than ever before, reacting within three hours. Targeting was done at I Corps and XXIV Corps. Since there was little ground followup to B-52 strikes, it was impossible to place a quantitative value on these missions, but ARVN ground officers were high in their praise of this powerful weapon, believing that it could wipe out everything in front of them and using it as a close support weapon. Prisoner reports and reports of ground commanders indicated that the B-52s caused heavy casualties and disrupted the enemy's capacity to strike at ARVN forces. When the enemy massed for the attack on Hill 31 on 21 February, an Arc Light strike was later credited by the FAC with having killed 698 enemy. Throughout the fighting in Lam Son 719, the B-52s were used to support air assaults on enemy objectives, prepare landing zones and clear a path for friendly advancing forces. 17/

Lam Son 719 proved conclusively that there was no substitute for a tactical fighter in knocking out a moving tank. The destruction of 74 tanks and the damaging of 24 more by tac air practically wiped out the enemy's armored regiment.[18] More important, as will be pointed out in Chapter III, it may have prevented a major disaster.

Night support to friendly forces was provided by AC-130 and AC-119 gunships and proved invaluable on numerous occasions. When Objective 31 was under attack in February, AC-130s and AC-119s were on continuous duty over the ARVN positions for three consecutive nights, taking a heavy toll of enemy attackers. During Lam Son 719, the USAF gunships flew 239 sorties, with more than one fourth of them flown during the last five days of the operation when the situation was critical.[19]

The role of the U.S. Army helicopters is discussed briefly later in this report. The performance of the helicopter crews in the midintensity environment of Lam Son 719 was truly exceptional, and they sustained the heaviest U.S. casualties of the operation in Laos. The Army had overestimated the capability of the helicopter to perform against the numerous enemy automatic weapons and the "barrage fire" technique used by enemy troops. This latter tactic made it extremely difficult for choppers to land on many bases. The enemy troops would deploy in rows, each firing continuously into the air, usually when the "slicks" came in to land. Early in the operation, the Army was convinced that they could fly at treetop level and sweep in unexpected at this low level on enemy fixed positions, but after the heavy losses of the first weeks, they soberly reappraised the helicopter role. The Army flew nearly 90,000 helicopter sorties in Lam Son 719, most of these troop lift and gunship sorties.*

About 2000 C-130 resupply sorties were flown, delivering personnel and cargo to Dong Ha, Quang Tri and the reconstructed base at Khe Sanh, which opened for sustained C-130 operations on 15 February after an abortive attempt to open a dirt assault strip on 4 February. There were major problems with construction of a satisfactory strip at Khe Sanh and building of a second strip with aluminum matting, reducing the C-130 traffic into the base and forcing greater Army use of Highway 9, running from Dong Ha on the coast to the inland base. Nevertheless, between 4 February and 23 March, C-130s hauled some 20,000 tons of cargo to support U.S. and ARVN units involved in the operation.

INTERIM ASSESSMENT OF AIR SUPPORT FOR LAM SON 719

The assessment of the role of air power in Lam Son 719 would require extensive analysis covering interdiction, suppression of AA fire, destruction of tanks, close air support to troops in contact and preparation of landing zones. These will be dealt with briefly here and in more detail in later chapters of this report.

---

*On a given mission, one helicopter might log five or more sorties, a sortie being defined as a take off from point A to a landing or a hovering attitude at point B.

INTERDICTION

Tactical and strategic air participation in Lam Son 719 was a continuation of an interdiction program, Commando Hunt V, focused on the Steel Tiger area of Laos which included the Lam Son 719 combat area. The difference was that a large ground force was to move into a key interdiction area, thus increasing interdiction effectiveness. At the focal point of the ARVN operation, the junction of Routes 9 and 92, there was effective ground interdiction for a short period. On Routes 92B and 92C, running north and south from Route 9 respectively, traffic came almost to a complete halt for two weeks after the ARVN force reached A Loui at the junction. Sensor-detected truck movements on Routes 92B and 92C showed over 200 and 300 movements, respectively, going north and south weekly in the three weeks prior to Lam Son 719. (See Figure 2.) This rate dropped to practically no detection on 92B and to only a handful of detections on 92C starting around the middle of February. However, traffic on Route 914, leading from just west of Tchepone south of the main ARVN force to Base Area 611, rose sharply in conjunction with the drop in 92 traffic. In January 1971, traffic on 914B averaged around 445 sensor-detected movements a week, rising sharply at the height of Lam Son 719 operations to 1226 movers in the week of 3-10 March, nearly a threefold increase. Enemy truck traffic on Route 1032B from the DMZ area to just north of the Lam Son 719 area (a main reinforcement route) continued high throughout the campaign, rising from only 16 sensor-detected truck movements in the first week of January to 646 movements in the week of 3-10 March, a week before the enemy's counterattack.[20] Seventh Air Force senior officers were anxious for the RVNAF to carry out its original plan of interdicting 914B and 914C as this obviously emerged as the main enemy alternate route.[21] A full report on the Commando Hunt V interdiction effort which includes the Lam Son 719 operation is being published separately and will shed additional light on overall interdiction effectiveness. Another CHECO report to be published on air operations in the Steel Tiger area of Laos will cover the interdiction efforts of a Lao irregular force to the south and west of Tchepone in an operation called DESERT RAT. This four battalion force, between 16 February and 23 March, sought to interdict Route 23 and 233 if Lam Son 719 pressure forced the enemy to use more westerly routes. The enemy was never forced to use these routes, but the DESERT RAT irregulars, supported by 58 USAF and 350 RLAF sorties, destroyed 39 trucks, damaged 11 more, created 221 secondary explosions and fires, cut 104 meters of road, and came within 18 miles of Tchepone from the west before withdrawing to the southwest.[22]

SUPPRESSION OF AA FIRE

The enemy had deployed throughout the Steel Tiger area an integrated mobile antiaircraft defense system including some 525-575 guns, mainly 37mm and 23mm with some 57mm weapons. In addition, he used artillery, tank and infantry weapons against low flying aircraft, mainly helicopters. SA-2 missiles were also deployed to attack aircraft, including B-52s flying over the area. A particularly effective antiaircraft tactic against helicopters was the use of barrage fire by deployed infantrymen around an

SENSOR DETECTED TRUCK MOVEMENTS IN LAM SON AREA*

Rtes	16-23 Dec	23-30 Dec	30 Dec-6 Jan	6-13 Jan	13-20 Jan	20-26 Jan	27Jan-3Feb	3-10 Feb	10-17 Feb	17-24 Feb	24Feb-3Mar	3-10 Mar	10-17 Mar	17-24 Mar	24-31 Mar	31Mar-7Apr
1032B	423	137	16	35	347	170	257	238	242	385	302	646	167	355	464	388
914B	390	190	198	585	428	372	397	593	1202	1357	602	1226	926	739	550	466
914C	186	178	137	296	264	166	177	302	430	525	311	435	276	137	255	126
92A	15	30	43	15	38	32	27	127	168	247	103	249	221	177	226	103
92B	123	108	57	80	228	218	261	253	43	0	0	3	2	5	4	28
92C	285	342	223	290	349	308	312	241	49	16	0	36	131	91	43	72
913	66	122	113	169	120	175	126	281	132	43	74	34	22	35	68	80

* For a more detailed analysis of sensor detections, see Logistics Movement Appendix.

FIGURE 2

ARVN base firing RPG, small arms, and 12.7mm machine guns simultaneously against helicopters coming in and out of a besieged area.[23]

The USAF, with previous experience against enemy AAA in this area, used a variety of ordnance to suppress the enemy fire. The CBU 24 was found not to be effective, because while it could knock out the enemy gunners, too often it would leave the gun there to be remanned by others. It was also difficult to knock out an AAA position with hard bombs, not only because of the need for a direct hit, but because of skillful enemy camouflage of bunkers. The laser-guided Paveway was the most effective weapon against antiaircraft artillery, providing almost 100 percent accuracy with a circular error average of five meters. During the period of this report, tac air destroyed 109 and damaged 18 AA sites.[24]

USE OF TAC AIR AGAINST ENEMY ARMOR

During Lam Son 719, the enemy was reported to have had between 120 and 200 tanks; there were 241 tac air attacks against this armor, resulting in 74 destroyed and 24 damaged. As indicated earlier in this chapter, this spectacular success may well have deprived the enemy of the one weapon which would have allowed him to inflict a disaster upon withdrawing ARVN forces in the latter stage of the operation. The three enemy tanks used in the operation were the PT-76, a light, thin-skinned amphibious tank, the T-34 medium tank, and the T-54 medium tank equipped with a 12.7mm machine gun and a 100mm cannon in its turret. Fighters used almost their complete range of weapons against enemy armor. A most effective weapon was the laser-guided bomb (MK84 LGB and M118 LGB) which destroyed seven

19

tanks in eight deliveries. The Rockeye MK 20 destroyed and damaged 7 tanks in 22 drops. AC-119 and AC-130 gunships with 20mm and 40mm guns destroyed 24 tanks in 39 attacks. The remainder of the tanks were knocked out with napalm, CBU, hard bombs and tac air 20mm fire. Army helicopters were credited with knocking out six enemy tanks during the operation.[25/] (See Figure 3.)

AIR SUPPORT IN LANDING ZONE PREPARATION

Preparation of landing zones in the Lam Son 719 area by tac air and B-52s was extremely important to the aerial mobility of ARVN forces. As mentioned earlier, in the early phase of the campaign, prior to the Lo Lo landing of 3 March, the Army did not recognize the requirement for intensive prep by tactical air prior to ARVN landings. However, following Lo Lo, tactical air was given more emphasis. A 7th AF concept for LZ prep called for Arc Light strikes during the night, C-130 Commando Vault drops at first light if required, followed by tactical air sorties using a variety of weapons, including smoke if necessary. This procedure meant that RVNAF units could not move into their objectives early in the day, whereas General Lam preferred to give his men as much daylight as possible to prepare night defenses. The increased emphasis on tactical air following Lo Lo reduced helicopter and troop losses although practically every landing zone and pickup zone in the Lam Son 719 area was subject to enemy fire from a force dispersed and prepared for such landings.[26/] (See Figure 4.)

Three Destroyed Tanks
(600 ft Southeast of Hill 31)
FIGURE 3

Bomb Damage Assessment/Overrun
of ARVN Strongpoints
(3.5NM West of Laos/RVN border)
FIGURE 4

Certainly in Lam Son 719, tactical air support linked with the massive firepower of the B-52 formed an essential and vital cover for the ARVN incursion and its withdrawal. Without the assurance that the friendly aircraft would be overhead and that the skies above Lam Son 719 would be free of enemy air, the operation would probably not even have been contemplated.

This chapter has reviewed the overall operation. The following chapter reviews some of the initial planning that went into the operation.

CHAPTER II

PLANNING FOR LAM SON 719

CONCEPT OF OPERATIONS

As originally conceived, Lam Son 719 was an operation designed to counter the achievement of North Vietnam's primary goal for 1971: to expand its lines of communication (LOC) to Cambodia and the Republic of Vietnam.[27/] This goal was not new, as the enemy had consistently striven to improve his Laos LOCs during the dry season each year. However, with the loss of his sea supply route to Cambodia via Kompong Som in 1970, his trail activity in Laos became more important to him in sustaining his operations. Therefore, the enemy reconstituted his traditional trail system in the eastern portion of the Laos panhandle. He also undertook some expansion of the system to the west, but he never used this additional capability to any appreciable extent.[28/]

The XXIV Corps Lam Son 719 Operation Order called for a coordinated air and ground attack along Route 9 into the enemy's Base Area 604 west and south of Tchepone. All enemy caches discovered were to be destroyed in place, not removed following their capture as in the Cambodian cross-border operation. To deny the enemy his sanctuaries in the area his LOCs were to be cut at Tchepone and the intersection of Routes 9 and 92.[29/] While search and destroy operations were being conducted in Base Area 604, the enemy's major routes to the north and south of Tchepone would be blocked. The ground action in Laos was to be the sole responsibility of the RVN forces, who would be supported by U.S. tactical air, B-52s, gunships, helicopters and artillery in this combined operation. The entire operation was originally planned to be conducted in four phases.

THE PLANNED PHASES

Phase I. This phase, commencing on D-Day, 30 January, called for the 1st Brigade (Bde) of the U.S. 5th Infantry Division supported by tac air to attack to the west so as to clear and secure Route 9 from Dong Ha to the western Quang Tri border and secure Vandegrift Fire Support Base (FSB) and Khe Sanh. At the same time the 1st Brigade was to cover and protect the deployment of two U.S. heavy artillery battalions to western Quang Tri Province and establish a screen southward to the Laotian salient.* Simultaneously, the U.S. 101st Airborne Division was to set up defensive positions to protect the central and eastern portions of the Demilitarized Zone (DMZ). An ARVN 1st Armored Bde Task Force was to follow the 1st Bde of the 5th Infantry Division and, after the capture of Khe Sanh, was to move to the northwest of Khe Sanh to screen the northern flank. 30/

An integral part of Phase I was concerned with prepositioning 6500 troops of the ARVN 1st Airborne Division and 3000 troops of a Vietnamese Marine Brigade. The plan was for the U.S. 834th Air Division to airlift these troops from the Saigon Area through Tan Son Nhut and Bien Hoa to the off-load bases of Quang Tri and Dong Ha in MR 1 during the period D+1

---

*For security purposes, and to confuse the enemy in event of leaks, Lam Son 719 areas of interest were given the names of locations in the A Shau Valley and the entire operations was initially referred to as Dewey Canyon II. Dewey Canyon I had been an earlier operation in the A Shau Valley.

through D+4. In addition, it was expected that about 200 airlift sorties would be needed to support U.S. forces in Phase I. Airlift operations were to be on a 24-hour-per-day basis through D+4 when normal daylight operations were to be resumed.[31/]

All of Phase I was expected to require five to eight days for completion.

Phase II. Under this phase, the South Vietnamese I Corps, supported and assisted by the U.S. XXIV Corps and 7AF tac air, was to attack rapidly to the west using both ground and air mobile operations to seize Tchepone. The first objective on the way to Tchepone was A Loui, the intersection of Routes 9 and 92. The ARVN 1st Airborne Division, with the 1st Armored Brigade attached to it, was to conduct the main attack along Route 9 as far as A Loui. Once A Loui had been secured, an airborne brigade of the ARVN 1st Airborne Division was to conduct heliborne operations from Khe Sanh in order to capture Tchepone. At the same time, the ARVN 1st Infantry Division was to conduct a series of heliborne operations to seize the high ground to the south of Route 9G between A Loui and Tchepone. The ARVN 1st Ranger Group was tasked with establishing blocking positions to provide security for the northern flank. One Vietnamese Marine Corps Brigade, initially in reserve, was to later conduct operations south of Khe Sanh and against the Laotian salient. Two days prior to the start of Phase II, U.S. tac air was to begin a concentrated AAA suppression campaign, to last from three to seven days, along Route 9G and in the vicinity of Tchepone.[32/]

Phase III. According to the XXIV Corps Operation Order for Lam Son 719, this phase was to start after the capture of Tchepone. Having consolidated their positions along Route 9 in the Lam Son area of operations, I Corps was to conduct systematic search and destroy operations in the enemy's Base Area 604 west and south of Tchepone. The 1st Airborne Division was then to establish blocking positions northwest of Tchepone along Route 91 and southeast of Tchepone along Route 9G so as to isolate the area. At the same time the 1st Infantry Division was to conduct search and destroy operations in its assigned area just to the south of the Xe Pon River while the 1st Ranger Group would continue its blocking and screening operations on the north flank. Throughout this phase, which was to last until the beginning of the southwest monsoon season, tac air was to support the search and destroy operations in Base Area 604 and the blocking positions along the LOCs.[33]

Phase IV. This phase, also supported by tac air, was to consist of the I Corps withdrawal from Base Area 604 under one of two options: either by (1) the Airborne Division withdrawing directly to the east along Route 9 to cover an attack to the Southeast in Base Area 611 by the 1st Infantry Division or (2) by both divisions attacking Base Area 611. Either option was to include the insertion of guerilla units and RVNAF elements to stay behind and harass the enemy in Base Areas 604 and 611. (See Figure 5.) Under Option I, the 1st Airborne Division would withdraw from its blocking positions to A Loui. It would then act as cover for the 1st Infantry Division south of the Xe Pon. The infantry would reorient to the southeast and attack through Base Area 611 on its way back to South Vietnam. Once again the 1st Ranger Group would continue its protection of the north flank. The 1st Armored Brigade in the vicinity of A Loui would withdraw to Khe Sanh on order and revert to a reserve status. The 1st Ranger Group on the north flank would also withdraw to Khe Sanh and come under the operational control of the 1st Armored Bde which would prepare a task force for an attack to the south on order. The 1st Airborne Division would leave its blocking positions, and either follow the 1st Infantry Division and support it in its attack through Base Area 611 or else withdraw along Route 9 to Khe Sanh. Also, under this option, two Vietnamese Marine Corps Bdes would attack Base Area 611.

Under Option 2 of the final phase, with both the Airborne and the Infantry Division attacking, the maneuver concept of the various elements would remain unchanged with one exception. The 1st Infantry Division and the 1st Airborne Division, after attacking through the western portion of Base Area 611, would turn north in an attack through the Laotian salient, rather than continue to the southeast. [34/]

A COMBINED OPERATION

Lam Son 719 was a combined operation, but it was combined in such a way as to have somewhat unique characteristics. Because the operation was conducted in Laos, the roles of the Republic of Vietnam and the United States were quite different from what had been the norm in the Republic. The United States operated under certain inviolable restrictions. U.S. personnel were not to operate on the ground in Laos, and therefore the RVN forces operated without U.S. advisors.

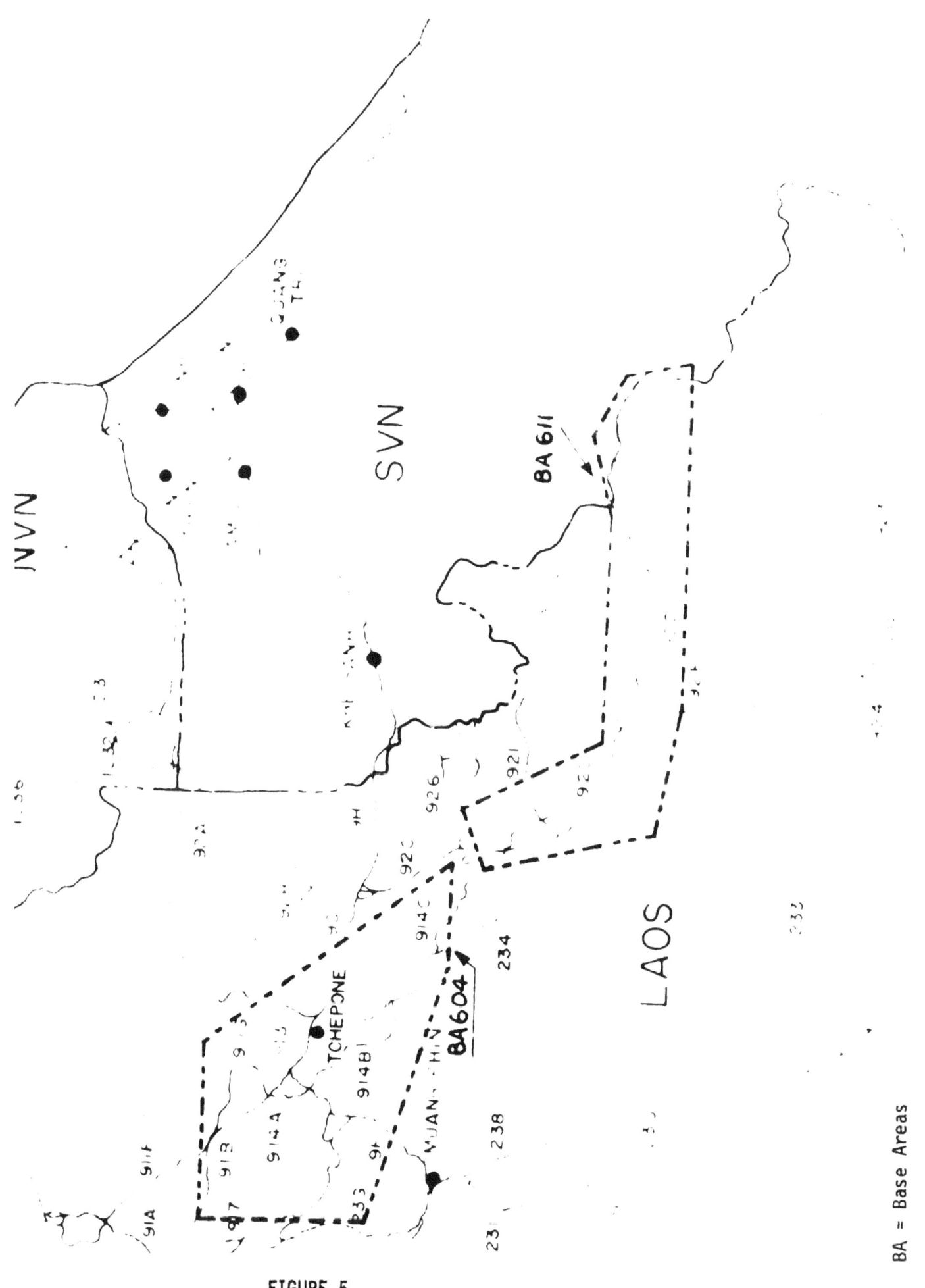

FIGURE 5

BA = Base Areas

The CG of ARVN I Corps, Lt General Hoang Xuan Lam, was in command of the ground campaign in Laos. COMUSMACV, General Creighton W. Abrams, of course, commanded all U.S. forces involved in the operation, and under him there were separate ground and air commanders. The CG of U.S. Army XXIV Corps, Lt General James W. Sutherland, commanded all U.S. Army forces in Military Region I of the RVN who were supporting Lam Son. The Commander of the 7AF, General Lucius D. Clay, Jr., commanded all supporting USAF resources. This command set up functioned effectively, but it was not without its problems in the areas of planning and appreciation for the use of tac air. [35]

Evidence of a lack of appreciation for the use of tac air occurred early in Phase II when the RVNAF actually crossed into Laos. Often ground tactical decisions relative to combat assaults were not announced in sufficient time to permit proper coordination of tac air strikes in preparing landing zones. (The preparation of landing zones is discussed in detail in Chapter IV of this report.) Briefly, General Lam chose not to coordinate his moves with XXIV Corps and DASC Victor. Seventh Air Force wanted not less than three hours to properly prepare a landing zone and counter the AA threat. However, General Lam was in favor of early morning insertions of his troops before the weather was good enough for tac air to bring its full power to bear. He, therefore, undertook insertions without prior coordination with XXIV Corps and DASC Victor and as a result suffered some rather severe losses. As will be shown later, when subsequent insertions were coordinated with the Air Force and tac air was given sufficient time to prepare a landing zone, losses were reduced. [36]

To improve planning and coordination, COMUSMACV on 3 March directed that a coordinating committee of general officers be established to act as a liaison and planning group between General Lam's I Corps Headquarters and XXIV Corps. The committee became operational on 6 March and consisted of a U.S. Army Brigadier General as an advisor for artillery, a U.S. Army Brigadier General as an advisor for Army aviation, a USAF Brigadier General as an advisor for tac air, and an ARVN Brigadier General as an advisor for ARVN artillery. Once established, that committee met with General Lam on a daily basis, and, in effect, served as additional staff for him to advise on all planned actions and to insure that coordination was effected with the various participating forces. The objective was to provide I Corps with the best possible support. 37/

CONTROL OF TACTICAL AIR

Procedures for the control of tactical air in support of the South Vietnamese ground forces participating in operations in Lam Son 719 were established by I DASC Operations Order 1-71. Under this plan, I DASC at Da Nang directed the required air support for Phase I of the operation through the established Tactical Air Control Parties (TACPs) within the RVN. For Phases II, III and IV; a new DASC, designated DASC Victor, was established at Quang Tri on 31 January to control air support for the RVNAF operating in Laos. This DASC became operational on 7 February. Forward air controllers from the 23d Tactical Air Support Squadron at Nakhon Phanom, Thailand -- call sign Nail -- were deployed to Quang Tri to provide the necessary FAC resources dedicated to air support of the ground forces in

28

Laos. Upon arrival at Quang Tri, these FACs were given the call sign Hammer, and it was through Hammer operations that DASC Victor controlled out-country air support. I DASC had Barky FACs at Quang Tri to provide air support for U.S. ground forces in Vietnam in Lam Son East. I DASC, as had been the case prior to the operation, remained under the control of the Tactical Air Control Center at 7AF Hq, while DASC Victor was under the control of the 7AF Command Post, Blue Chip.[38/] (See Figure 6.)

Another integral part of the control net was the 7AF Airborne Battlefield Command and Control Center (ABCCC), call sign Hillsboro/Moonbeam, which controlled air space over Laos. In Lam Son 719, the priority task of the ABCCC was to serve as a coordinating facility which accepted supporting tac air and then handed it off to a FAC for use in the area of operations. DASC Victor had operational control over the Hammer FACs. The DASC assigned the FACs to their various sectors, briefed them as to the location of known or possible targets, and passed in-flight advisories to them. The DASC also established priority on air for a particular FAC, but the ground situation changed so frequently that the FACs often had to coordinate changes in priority through the ABCCC and on occasion amongst themselves. In practice the FACs decided where to put the air strikes depending on the tactical situation at any given time.[39/]

Initial discussions between representatives of XXIV Corps, I Corps and 7AF were held in mid-January to develop the concept and procedures for air support in Lam Son 719. At that time I Corps indicated that they would employ two divisions plus two separate brigades. One force was to be located north of Route 9, one astride Route 9, and the other to the south of Route 9. Division Tactical Operation Centers (DTOCs) were to be located in Laos. With the DTOCs so located this would have meant that Air Force TACPs (to transmit ground requests to the FACs) could not have been located with the DTOCs because of the prohibition against U.S. forces on the ground in Laos. Therefore, it was decided that English-speaking Vietnamese observers would be assigned to FAC aircraft to translate as required. On 23 January, I Corps announced that its DTOCs would be located in the RVN in the vicinity of Khe Sanh, and it was then possible to establish TACPs at the same locations, thus simplifying communication procedures. However, it was decided to retain the English-speaking Vietnamese observers to assist the FACs in communicating with the individual ground commanders that they would be supporting.[40/] To support I Corps, 7AF provided FACs for each main force operating area with a planned stream of tactical air for each area. A stream was to consist of a set (two) of fighters every fifteen minutes.

On 27 January, three days prior to D-Day, the I Corps Commander notified DASC Victor that he would be employing three division-size forces--the 1st Airborne, the 1st Infantry and the Marine Division. At this point, another TACP was established, collocated with the additional DTOC in the vicinity of Khe Sanh. Throughout the operation there were three DTOCs, each with a TACP.

Requests for immediate air came up through RVNAF command channels to a DTOC where they were relayed to an Air Force liaison officer in a

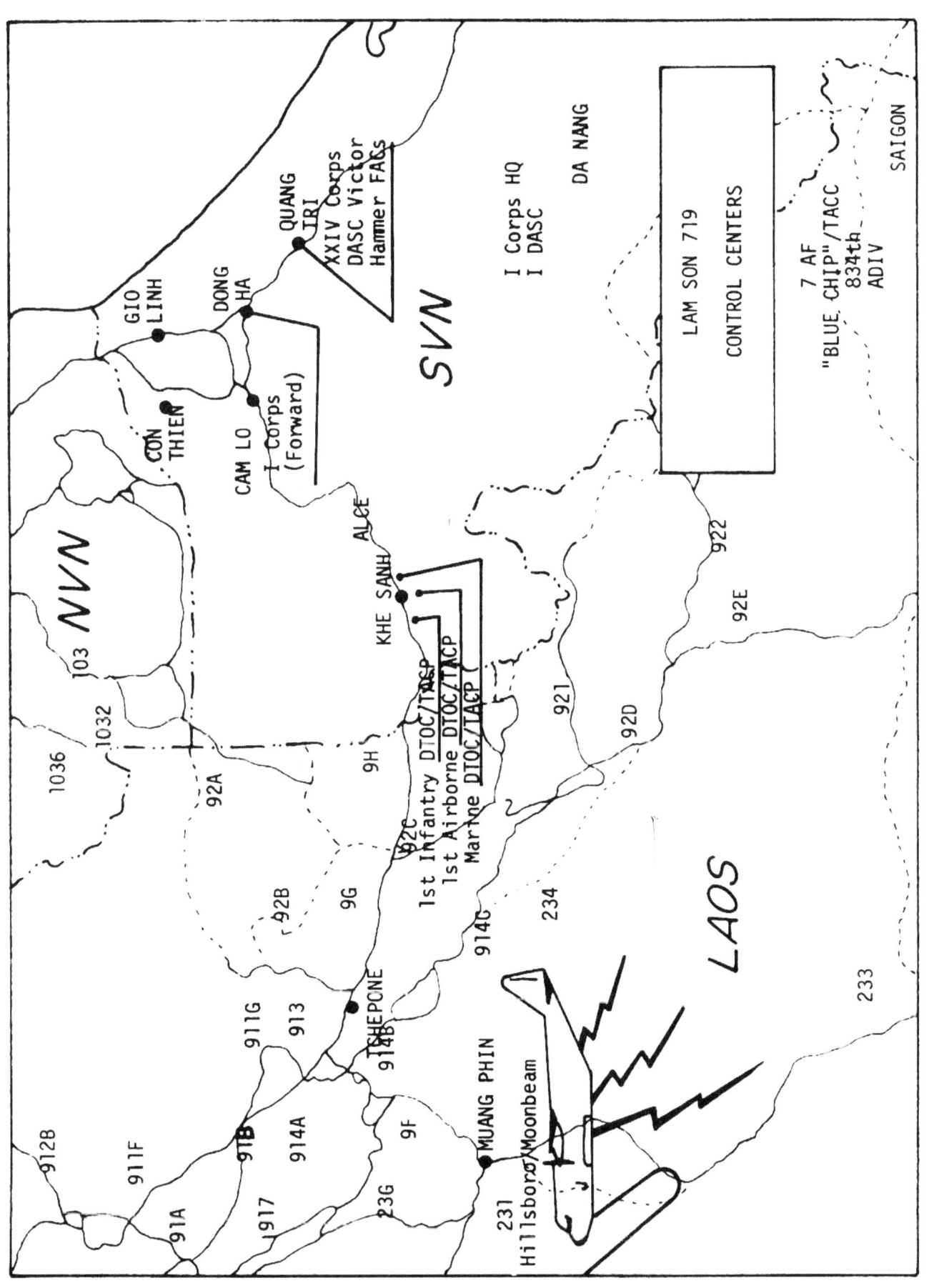

FIGURE 6

TACP, and from him directly to an airborne FAC or else through Victor DASC to a FAC, depending on the urgency of the ground situation. The FAC also received immediate requests directly from ground units in contact with the enemy. If the FAC had air available from the preplanned stream of air being fed to him by the ABCCC, he could use this resource to fill the request. If he needed additional air, he could coordinate with the ABCCC and obtain air in that way. In filling the request, the ABCCC could divert other preplanned air in the Steel Tiger interdiction area or air in the stream to the FAC, or request a scramble from Blue Chip depending on the urgency of the situation. Priorities to be used by the FACs in determining the urgency of requests were: (1) troops in contact (TIC), (2) search and rescue, (3) preplanned targets, (4) visual reconnaissance and (5) other missions requested by ground commanders.[41/]

Requests for preplanned air support flowed through the DTOCs to I DASC at Da Nang. I DASC then forwarded the preplanned requests to DASC Victor so as to arrive there no later than 1000 hours on any given day. From DASC Victor these requests were forwarded to 7AF where they were incorporated into the fragmentary orders for the next day's activity.[42/]

Lam Son 719 opened in Laos with Hammer FACs and streams of air assigned to each Division area, with a set of fighters every fifteen minutes in each stream. As the RVNAF area of operations enlarged, and the action became more intense, the number of FACs was raised to six, with each FAC being assigned his own sector to work. (As noted in Chapter I, there was an additional roaming FAC to act as an artillery spotter.) The increased demands for tac air also led to the reduction of the time intervals between sets of fighters to ten minutes or less. Six FACs became the norm for the operation. Senior XXIV Corps officers frequently wanted to raise the number of FACs assigned to the Area of Operation (AO), but because of the small size of the AO, 7AF felt that six was the maximum safe number for sustained day-to-day operations.

The AO, of course, was determined by the disposition of the friendly troops on the ground. A line parallel to the AO and five miles beyond it was established as a "no bomb" line. Within this NBL, all air strikes were controlled by the Hammer FACs in their various sectors. The total area inside the NBL at its largest was less than 700 square miles. With multiple fast-moving fighters in the area, six FACs, periodic Arc Light sorties, and Army helicopters operating in the area, tight command and control procedures were required. Seventh Air Force felt that to introduce additional aircraft would have been counterproductive. Furthermore, additional FACs would not have added to the number of available tac air sorties; the area of operation just could not accommodate any more aircraft. 43/

FORCES COMMITTED

Friendly Air. Air support for Lam Son 719 came from many different units.*
The 8th Tactical Fighter Wing (TFW) at Ubon Royal Thai Air Force Base (RTAFB), the 12th TFW at Phu Cat, and the 366th TFW at Da Nang all supplied F-4 strike sorties. The 460th Tactical Reconnaissance Wing (TRW) at Tan Son Nhut

---

*Units listed here are the ones with the major supporting roles. There are many other units involved on a smaller scale.

provided RF-4Cs for recce missions. F-100 sorties came from the 35th TFW at Phan Rang. The 1st Marine Air Wing at Da Nang launched F-4, A-4 and A-6 strikes while the Navy Carrier Task Force in the Gulf of Tonkin provided A-4, A-6, A-7 and F-4 strikes. The 56th Special Operations Wing (SOW) at Nakhon Phanom RTAFB was the source of A-1 aircraft for search and rescue. The 18th Special Operations Squadron, also at Nakhon Phanom supplied AC-119K gunships, and the 16th Special Operations Squadron at Ubon RTAFB supplied AC-130A gunships. FACs for the operation came from the 504th Tactical Air Support Group at Cam Ranh Bay through its several Tactical Air Support Squadrons. The 834th Air Division at Tan Son Nhut provided all required airlift with assigned C-130 and C-123 aircraft. The ABCCC aircraft came from the 7th Airborne Command and Control Squadron of the 432d TRW at Udorn RTAFB. The Strategic Air Command, through its 307th Strategic Wing at U-Tapao, provided B-52s and KC-135s. The VNAF provided fixed wing strike aircraft and transport helicopters from the 1st Air Division. Six VNAF Tactical Air Control Parties were established to support ARVN units.

Friendly Ground Forces. As noted earlier, the U.S. Army XXIV Corps, though not operating on the ground in Laos, did provide significant support for the RVNAF. The 108th Artillery Group provided supporting fires while the 45th Engineering Group rendered engineering support. The 101st Airborne Division (Airmobile) was the units which provided all U.S. helicopter support and made it possible for the RVNAF to undertake heliborne operations. The 1st Brigade of the 5th Infantry Division (Reinforced) protected the Lam Son 719 northern flank just below the DMZ.

The RVN I Corps main forces participating in Lam Son 719 were the 1st Airborne Division, the 1st Infantry Division, the Marine Division, the 1st Ranger Group, the 1st Armored Brigade and the 10th Engineering Group. Not all of these units were on the ground in Laos at the same time, and some of their elements did not cross the border. The maximum number of friendly maneuver and support troops in Laos at any one time was approximately 17,000.

Enemy Forces. It was estimated that the maximum number of enemy forces committed at any one time was 35,000. Of this figure, 24,000 were believed to be maneuver and combat support troops, with 11,000 being rear service personnel.[44/] From his B-5 front the enemy committed three infantry regiments and two artillery regiments.* From the 70B Corps, he employed two infantry regiments from the 304th Division and three infantry regiments from the 308th Division. He also used one infantry regiment from the 320th Division and two infantry regiments from the 2d Division and at least two infantry regiments from the 324B Division. The enemy also committed an unidentified tank regiment, at least two artillery regiments not associated with any of the units already mentioned, and at least nineteen antiaircraft battalions.

---

*It was difficult to determine accurately what units the enemy forces came from. Figures given here are best estimates based on various messages from General Abrams to General Clay.

CHAPTER III

THE CAMPAIGN

Operation Lam Son 719 began, as all planned offensives, with a deployment and build-up phase. U.S. forces were given the task of providing the logistical support and a secure rear area for the ARVN incursion forces. For the incursion to reap the benefits of tactical surprise, the preparation phase had to be executed quickly, efficiently and with a diversionary cover.

DEPLOYMENT OF U.S. FORCES

The First Brigade, Fifth Infantry Division (Mechanized) was given the primary combat role of providing security for the 45th Engineer Group which reconstructed Highway 9 within RVN, the fire support bases and the Khe Sanh combat support base. 45/

Operation Lam Son 719 actually began at 0001H on 30 January 1971 when lead elements of the First Brigade, Fifth Infantry Division attacked west from Fire Support Base Vandegrift along Highway 9. As the Third Squadron, Fifth Cavalry advanced along the road, engineers of the 14th Engineer Battalion installed nine tactical bridges and nine culverts. 46/

At 0830H, 30 January, three infantry battalions began a combat assault by helicopter into Khe Sanh. 47/ The assault was completed at 1530H without enemy contact. Simultaneously, the 101st Airborne Division (AML) conducted diversionary moves from FSB Bastogne to FSB Veghel then to FSB Zon, from which heavy artillery fire was directed into the A Shau Valley. Tactical air strikes and B-52 strikes supported these maneuvers.

By 1230H on 31 January Route 9 was open from Dong Ha to Khe Sanh for tracked vehicles and lightweight wheeled vehicles.[48/] The Task Force moved on towards the Laotian border, reaching it at 0800H on 3 February 1971.[49/] The First Brigade then sent armor and infantry task forces on sweeps to the north of Route 9 and south of Khe Sanh toward the Laotian salient. The engineers continued to work on QL9 and on 31 January began the preparation of an assault airstrip at Khe Sanh to accommodate C-130 aircraft.

AIRLIFT EFFORT

The airlift of U.S. troops and equipment into Military Region I to provide air and ground support for the Lam Son operation began on 26 January and continued through 6 February. This deployment required 320 sorties to lift the 2031 passengers and 2541.6 short tons of cargo. The in-country C-130 fleet was augmented with ten additional aircraft from its "off-shore" wings bringing the number of C-130 aircraft in Vietnam to 58. The entire fleet was initially utilized on an around-the-clock basis when the movement of the Vietnamese contingency forces began on 30 January 1971. The movement of the ARVN 1st Airborne Division and the 258th Vietnamese Marine Brigade from Tan Son Nhut Airfield to the Military Region I bases at Dong Ha and Quang Tri occurred between 30 January and 6 February with 247 sorties airlifting 9254 passengers and 1703.5 short tons of cargo. Subsequent to the initial deployment of forces, airlift operations into Khe Sanh were conducted at the rate of 40 sorties per day during the daylight hours, lifting more than 500 short tons a day.

The Dong Ha airfield had been closed for seven months and had to be reactivated for this operation. To support the airdrome operations, the 834th Air Division directed the positioning of several USAF units at Dong Ha. These included a Combat Control Team for communications and air traffic control and a Mobility Team to handle the offload of passengers and cargo. Also, it was necessary to install a Ground Control Approach system, temporary airfield lighting and a TACAN to permit all-weather, 24-hour-a-day operations.

The C-130 operations into Khe Sanh posed difficult and persistent problems throughout the campaign. The Army engineers completed the construction of a new assault landing strip on 4 February. The first C-130 aircraft landed on that day. (See Figure 7.) It was apparent that the dirt surface was too soft for sustained C-130 operations when the lightly loaded aircraft sank into it more than six inches. Consequently, it was recommended to the XXIV Corps Commander that the strip be surfaced with aluminum matting. The recommendation was approved and the engineers completed the matting of the assault strip on 15 February. Concurrently, repairs were being made on the old 3900-foot landing strip which was pocked with shell craters from the 1968 battles. Not until 1 March were the repairs on this longer runway completed.

When the 834th Air Division was brought into the airlift planning for Operation Lam Son 719, their planners learned that the Khe Sanh Combat Support Base was surrounded by artillery fire zones. In order to accommodate the proposed airlift operation, it was necessary to establish artillery fire corridors through the area for the transport aircraft. Coordination was effected with the XXIV Corps Artillery Officer and the air control agencies serving MR I, to create a corridor from Hue, a terminal control zone at Khe Sanh and an exit corridor to Quang Tri. Procedures were developed to permit the transports continuous access to the corridors during the daylight hours and for closure of the corridors in the event of a tactical emergency requiring that the artillery fire through or into them.

Although the Khe Sanh airfield was the responsibility of the U.S. Army and an Army Aviation Facilities unit was in place on the airfield, the airdrome facilities were not adequate to meet Air Force needs for all-weather, round-the-clock operations. Consequently, the USAF 1st Mobile Communications Group installed, maintained and operated a GCA unit, control tower, TACAN, plus runway and approach lighting. To insure rapid, efficient cargo handling and C-130 turn-around, the 834th Air Division sent to Khe Sanh a Combat Control Team (one officer, two airmen), a Mobility Team (one officer, 15 airmen), a Transportable Airlift Control Element (one officer, three airmen) and a maintenance turn-around team of three airmen. The Mobility Team was equipped with adverse terrain fork lifts and able to unload an aircraft fully loaded with palletized cargo in less than five minutes. During peak operations a C-130 was arriving

First C-130 to land at Khe Sanh in
support of Lam Son 719
FIGURE 7

ARVN Fire Support Base
(12NM East of Tchepone)
Figure 8

on an average of one every eight minutes. This sortie effort was sustained primarily by positioning 11 aircraft with supporting equipment and personnel including aircrews at Da Nang under a special airlift headquarters. However, until 15 February when the matting of the assault landing strip was finished and the C-130 resupply operations into Khe Sanh began, the burden of the logistics build-up was carried by the U.S. Army truck convoys over QL9 from Dong Ha and Quang Tri. 50/

A capability for the airdrop of ammunition, rations and POL to the South Vietnamese units operating in Laos was maintained throughout the operation. In keeping with the ground scheme of maneuver, the airdrop contingency plan provided for a two-mile wide artillery-free air corridor over Route 9 from Khe Sanh to Tchepone. A TACAN was installed by the 1st Mobile Communications Group for navigation in the corridor. The TACAN was located five miles southwest of Khe Sanh. Arrangements were made with I Corps G4 for the establishment of drop zones along Route 9 within the corridor. Supplies were stockpiled and rigged at Da Nang for this contingency. Procedures were developed with DASC V, the ABCCC and the artillery units for the implementation of the plan and communications were set up between the artillery and the air traffic control agencies for placing the artillery free corridor in effect. However, when the scheme of maneuver became one based on fixed fire support bases, resupply was accomplished by helicopters. The airlift contingency plan for fixed wing resupply in Laos was never used.

ARVN ASSEMBLY

During the deployment phase, selected ARVN units of I Corps including the 1st Armored Brigade, the 1st Ranger Group, two regiments of the 1st Infantry Division, two engineer battalions and small combat support units moved to the Khe Sanh area. There they were joined by the 1st Airborne Division and the 258th Marine Brigade. Vietnamese units joined in the searching operations of the U.S. task forces and prepared for the attack into Laos.

The first contact with the enemy came on 4 February when a U.S. engineer unit was attacked 24 kilometers northwest of Khe Sanh. Elements of the 2d Squadron, 17th Air Cavalry engaged the enemy force killing five of them. Enemy contact remained light through 7 February.

Preparations for the invasion culminated when tactical air strikes and artillery fires were put on targets in Laos in preparation for the initial helicopter assaults. The 14 tactical air strikes requested for this purpose were directed at suspected antiaircraft artillery positions rather than the landing zone areas. These targets were selected by the ground commanders. Additionally, 20 strikes were placed on interdiction points along Route 9 beyond Ban Dong and about Tchepone. On early 8 February seven B-52 strikes were made in support of the ARVN invasion force. [51/]

JUMP-OFF

At 1000H on 8 February, the 2d Troop of the 17th Armored Cavalry Squadron (ARVN) crossed the border into Laos as lead element of the 1st Armored Task Force. No enemy contact was reported. [52/]

The 4th Bn, 3rd Inf Regiment, and 3rd Infantry Regiment Command Post completed a heliborne combat assault into LZ Hotel at 1045H. There was no contact with the enemy. The weather in this area was described as fair to good with a cloud ceiling of 3,000 feet and the cloud coverage was "broken." [53]

The 21st Ranger Battalion completed a combat assault into high ground overlooking Route 925 and the Namxe Samou River, closing at 1500H. On landing, the unit received 12.7mm machine gun fire wounding 11 rangers. The enemy was obviously present in this area. U.S. Air Cavalry gunships covering the helicopter troop lift killed one enemy soldier, destroyed two trucks and fired on an enemy bunker complex causing numerous secondary explosions lasting 30 minutes after the attack. [54] The rangers moved from the LZ to take up positions three kilometers to the east on the ridge line and begin screening operations on the northern flanks. [55]

Simultaneously with the rangers' assault, the 2d Airborne Battalion was lifted to a landing site two kilometers east of Objective 30. They arrived at Objective 30 at 1125H. No enemy opposition was encountered.

The initial combat assault of the 1st Airborne Division was complete at 1700H when the 3d Airborne Battalion and 3d Airborne Brigade closed Objective 31. The airborne battalions immediately began to dig in and to construct fire support bases on the two hills. [56]

The southwesterly thrust of the 1st Infantry Division was completed for the day when the 1st and 2d Battalions, 3d Infantry Regiment landed near LZ Blue, eight kilometers southwest of LZ Hotel. Both battalions received small arms and automatic weapons fire in the landing zone area. 57/

In the center, the Armored Task Force had moved ten kilometers west on Route 9 by 1130H and remained in this location overnight. The highway was in poor condition with numerous washouts, and the dense underbrush on the sides hampered the progress of the two airborne infantry battalions screening for the armored column. 58/

Thus the attack was launched and by nightfall 6,200 Vietnamese troops were in Laos. 59/ The costs of the first day's combat were light for the ARVN with three killed in action and 38 wounded and three missing in action. Three UH-1H helicopters were shot down by enemy gunners and several others suffered combat damage.

The weather conditions had been marginal in the operational area resulting in some tac air missions being diverted because of low ceilings and poor visibility. In these cases, the fire support was provided by artillery units. 60/

DRIVE TO A LOUI

The weather deteriorated further on 9 February forcing postponement of the planned helicopter combat assaults. The ground combat operations progressed satisfactorily; however, the road improvement efforts of the ARVN engineers were severely hampered by the rain.

The poor condition of Route 9 held the 1st Armored Task Force's advance to only five kilometers for the day. The other ARVN units improved their fire support bases and conducted patrols in the vicinity of the initial LZs. At 0520H on 10 February a patrol of the 21st Ranger Battalion sighted three enemy tanks and other vehicles towing artillery pieces moving on the road north of their position. The Rangers set up a road block and requested tactical air strikes. However, low ceilings and poor visibility prevented the fighters from engaging the targets. Helicopter gunships were employed but were unsuccessful in destroying the tanks. Contact with the enemy was concentrated in the Ranger area but even here it was light. The enemy appeared to be protecting his assets and natt   According to a FAC report, some enemy   ned positions near Objective A Loui. Elev   were seen moving west on Route 9. Tactic   ..res were employed with unknown results. 61/

Low ceilings and poor visibility on 10 February delayed the helicopter assault of additional battalions until afternoon. Further, both LZs were defended. Helicopter gunships preparing LZ Delta received 12.7mm machine gun and small-arms fire. One OH-6 and one AH-1 were downed. Both crews were extracted and preparations continued. The first lift of the 4th Battalion, 1st Infantry Regiment, landed at 1507H with the assault completed at 1632H. 62/

The initial lift of the 9th Airborne Battalion into the LZ at Objective A Loui was delayed by heavy antiaircraft fire. The LZ was defended by five truck-mounted 12.7mm machine guns and small arms. Helicopter gunships and USAF fighters were employed to suppress the enemy guns. The lead elements of the battalion began touching down at 1515H and the entire battalion had been delivered by 1720H. [63]

The Armored Task Force reached the intersection of Routes 9 and 92 at 1500H. Elements immediately began to secure the A Loui landing zone. Link-up between the 9th Airborne and the 1st Armored Brigade was then effected. Armored Cavalry elements reconnoitered Route 9 west of A Loui and reported it in very good condition, capable of sustaining speeds of 35 mph. [64]

Earlier in the day a disaster had befallen the ARVN Command when the I Corps' G3 and G4 were killed in a VNAF helicopter that crashed over the battle zone after receiving 37mm artillery fire. [65]

With the addition of two more infantry battalions into Laos, the Vietnamese strength rose to 7500 men. The build-up of troops continued on 11 February.

The 39th Ranger Battalion was heli-lifted to a landing zone near the 21st Ranger's position. Their lift was uneventful and completed in two hours having started at 1035H. [66]

Two battalions of the 1st Infantry Regiment made a combat assault into LZ Don. The third wave of helicopters lifting the 3d Battalion came under 12.7mm machine gun fire and the assault was temporarily delayed while helicopter gunships placed suppressing fire in the area. The First Battalion was diverted from LZ White to reinforce the 3d Battalion at LZ Don after the ARVN command received a report of a large enemy force located six kilometers south of the landing zone. This lift was completed at 1730H. Five hours earlier the 1st Infantry Regiment headquarters and two batteries had arrived by helicopter at FSB Delta. 67/

During the day the Armored Task Force sent motorized patrols three kilometers north and three kilometers south of A Loui on Route 92. These patrols established road blocks, one of which engaged an enemy force resulting in one ARVN soldier killed, one wounded and two armored personnel carriers destroyed. 68/

The 21st Ranger Battalion position overlooking Route 925 received two attacks-by-fire, each consisting of 40 rounds of 82mm mortars, during the night of 11-12 February. Six rangers were wounded. 69/

CONSOLIDATION

At 1000H on 12 February the 2d Battalion, 1st Infantry Regiment, began a helicopter lift into FSB Delta. The lift was completed at noon and followed by the lift of an engineer platoon with two D-2 bulldozers for improvement of the fire support base. 70/ At each of the other fire support bases--Hotel, A Loui, Alpha, Hills 30 and 31 and Ranger Hill--the ARVN soldiers improved and expanded the defenses about the artillery batteries and command post bunkers. All but A Loui, were on high ground and all had a commanding position overlooking an enemy avenue of travel. Later, this was to be as dangerous tactically as it was now advantageous.

SEARCHING FOR CACHES

The ARVN began searching operations about their increasingly elaborate defensive positions. The 3d Battalion, 1st Infantry Regiment searching near FSB Delta found a weapons and POL cache which contained 60 SKS rifles, 202 AK-47 rifles, four AA machine guns, large quantities of ammunition, 500 boxes of uniforms and 16,400 liters of POL. The 2d Troop, 17th Armored Cavalry Squadron on a search operation found 50 enemy bodies believed to have been killed by artillery or airstrikes. It was estimated that they had been dead for two to three days. Elements of the 3d Airborne and 1st Bn, 1st Infantry, each found sizable caches. 71/

Elements of the Armored Task Force proceeded west on Route 9 to a point five kilometers beyond FSB A Loui. Further westward movement was to be keyed to resumption of the airmobile assault along the northern ridge which never came.

The South Vietnamese forces in Laos now totaled more than 10,000 men in thirteen infantry battalions, two ranger battalions, two artillery battalions and one engineer battalion. 72/

This force was deployed in positions forming an elongated crescent along Route 925 on the northern flank, south along Route 92, southeastward to Route 926 and the RVN-Laos border. The center of the line was FSB A Loui on Route 9 in the five kilometer-wide Xe Pon River Valley with the right flank on the ridgeline of the 2,000-foot hills to the north of the valley and the left flank on the high ground to the south of the steep escarpment which forms the southern wall of the valley. The hills above the valley are heavily forested and broken by numerous streams and valleys. The ARVN drive to Tchepone temporarily lost its westward momentum as the units searched for caches by day and defended their fire support bases by night.

Through the daylight hours of 13 and 14 February, the ARVN searching parties found truck parks, POL storage areas, food caches, ammunition dumps and small base camps. They found it tactically desirable to call in tactical air strikes to destroy the finds. A particular spectacular result of tactical air strikes on caches was witnessed by patrols of the 21st and 39th Ranger Battalions. They had passed the coordinates of suspected storage areas to their DTOC which in turn passed them to the FAC working the Ranger area for use as targets of opportunity. The area eight kilometers north of FSB 30 was hit by five sets of fighters over an eight-hour period on 14 February. The Rangers reported observing five ammunition dumps burning and estimated the cumulative destruction at 304 tons of ammunition.[73] Dense smoke covered the area for hours.

Eighty-four sorties were flown on 13 February and 97 on 14 February by USAF fighters and gunships in support of the ARVN troops. Most of the daylight strikes were against storage areas, enemy troop concentrations, or enemy artillery positions. The night sorties predominantly supported ARVN troops in direct contact with enemy forces.

Each night three FACs, three flareships (C-123) and three gunships (AC-119 or AC-130), one of each for the Rangers, the Airborne Division and the Infantry Division were on station all the time. The Ranger positions were under almost continuous attack in the early morning hours of 13 and 14 February for they were sitting in the middle of a sizable storage area and closest to the enemy's troop concentration. The enemy attackers got as close as possible to the friendly perimeters in an attempt to minimize the effectiveness of the gunships and fighter strikes. The weather was clear both nights and continuous air coverage was provided.

The B-52 Arc Light strikes in these early days of the invasion were against I Corps selected targets such as enemy artillery emplacements, known storage areas and suspected enemy troop positions. The use of Arc Light strikes to support ARVN troops in contact with the enemy was made on 14 February for the first time.[74] More will be said about this technique as the campaign progresses.

Though all ARVN fixed positions received some attacks by fire, the Rangers experienced the heaviest pressure because of their proximity to the enemy's major forces.

ENEMY TROOP DISPOSITION

When the ARVN forces crossed the border into Laos it was estimated that there were about 23,000 North Vietnamese and Pathet Lao troops in the Laotian Military Regions III and IV. Subsequently the estimate was 15,000 maneuver and combat support troops and 12,000 rear service personnel facing the friendly units in the Lam Son 719 area of operation. Later these figures were again revised to 24,000 and 11,000 respectively.

The 70B Corps with three infantry divisions employing artillery ranging from 105mm to 240mm and a tank regiment with 120 vehicles including T-54s operated in the area from Khe Sanh to southern Laos. Its three divisions had specific areas of responsibility within the Corps region. The 308th Division operated from Khe Sanh to the RVN-Laos border and in mid-February had only one regiment engaged with others enroute. The 304th Division had the responsibility for the area from the border west to A Loui with the 24B Regiment and advance elements of the 66th and possibly the 9th Regiments. The 320th Division with only the 64th Regiment assigned in mid-February operated west of A Loui. The bulk of the 70B Corps forces were north of Route 9 and faced the northern portion of the ARVN line. Additionally, the 102d Regiment (Reinforced) was located north of Route 925 opposite the ARVN Ranger elements.

Elements of the 2d NVA Division and Rear Service units opposed the ARVN 1st Infantry positions on the southern flank and were concentrated along Routes 914 and 921. Later in February, the 324B Division moved into the Laotian salient and joined with the 2d Division and Rear Service units to put heavy pressure on the ARVN 1st Infantry Division and the VNMC Brigades. 75/ (See Figure 9.)

In the Republic of Vietnam, the B-5 Front with the 31st and 27th Infantry Regiments, 84th and 38th Artillery Regiments and the 15th Engineer

Battalion, operated between Dong Ha and Khe Sanh with the mission of harassing U.S. forces and cutting the allied LOC.[76]

The Communist forces from 10-16 February reacted to the invasion with an ever increasing volume of artillery and rocket attacks against the fire support bases from Dong Ha to A Loui. Every one of them was hit several times.[77]

SCREENING TECHNIQUES OF U.S. FORCES

In Quang Tri Province, which was the responsibility of the U.S. forces, the 1st Brigade, 5th Infantry, employed a highly effective technique which capitalized on air mobility and massive firepower. Small combat teams were moved from one terrain feature to another throughout the AO. When one of the teams located an enemy force it immediately requested artillery fire, helicopter aerial rocket artillery (ARA) and tactical air strikes. When a sizable enemy force was fixed, the teams reassembled into squads and platoons and fought on the company level under the control of the battalion commander. Employing this technique in one engagement on 15 February near FSB Vandegrift, 115 enemy were killed. Using highly mobile combat teams with fire support enabled the First Brigade to maintain the security of this rather large AO.[78]

ARVN TACTICS

The ARVN forces also relied heavily on the massive array of U.S. firepower available to them in the form of artillery, aerial rocket artillery, gunships, B-52s and tactical fighters. However, they did not employ the same

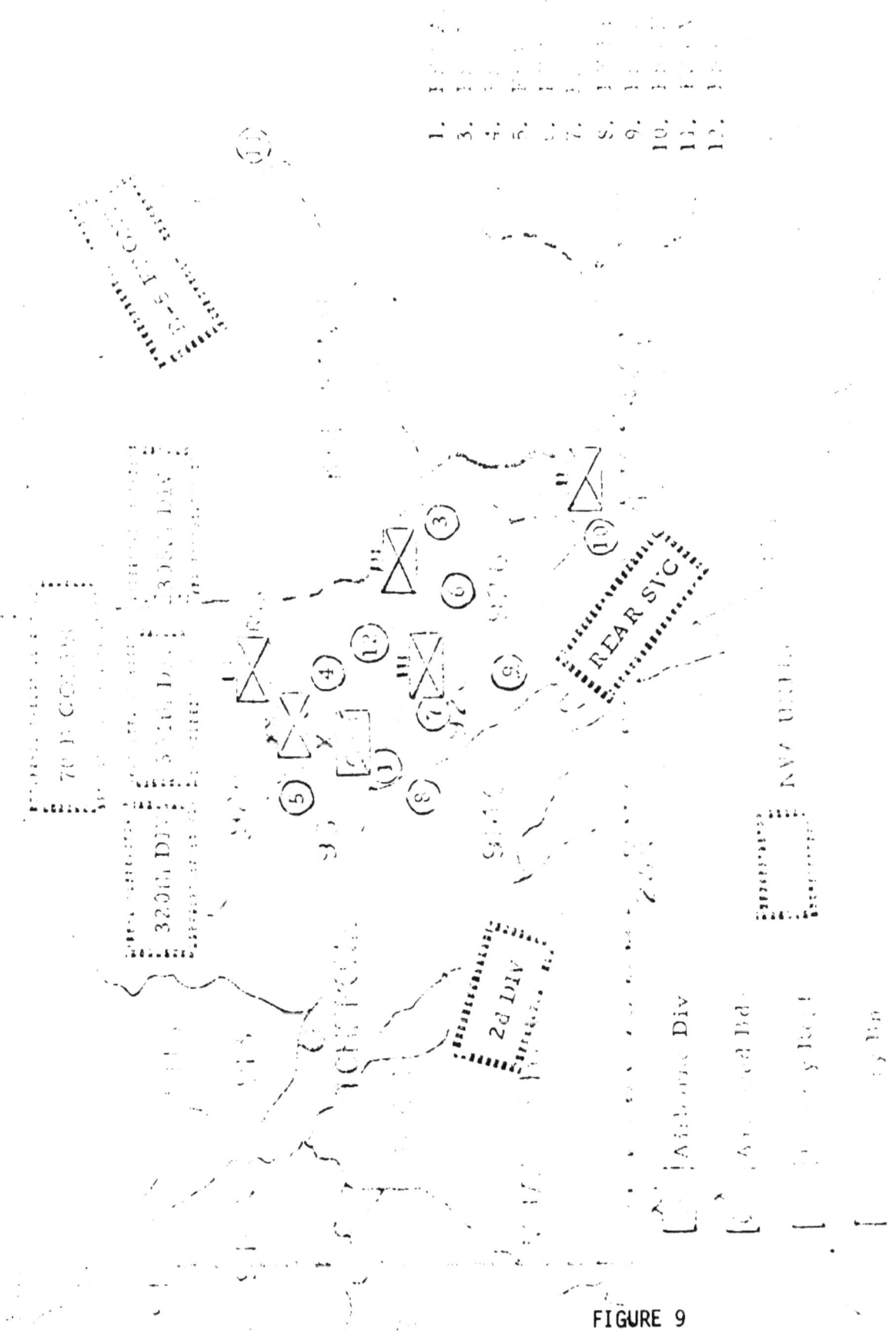

FIGURE 9

techniques of highly mobile teams constantly searching the area of operations. By 15 February, it was clear that the ARVN units, especially the Ranger and Airborne Battalions, preferred to operate close to their fire support bases and to search in platoon or company size elements. This was less true of the 1st Infantry Division whose battalions were more experienced in the terrain and the NVA tactics than their Airborne and Ranger compatriots. Elements of the 3d Infantry Regiment searched far south from FSB Hotel and all 1st Infantry Division units sent out night patrols to set ambushes on the approaches to their fire support bases.[79/]

The introduction of the 6th Airborne Battalion into Objective 31 on 13 February brought RVNAF strength in Laos to 10,288. The searching operations continued with relatively light enemy contact through 17 February. On this day the 2d Battalion, 3d Infantry Regiment in a thrust towards Base Area 611 moved south to Route 921 interdicting the road and destroying caches.

RANGER HILL

About midnight on 18 February, the 39th Ranger Battalion was attacked by a two-battalion-size enemy force. Several of the defensive outposts were overrun. U.S. artillery, flareships and gunships supported the defenders throughout the night. However, the fighting went on through the day and night of 19 February. The enemy breached the perimeter defenses and occupied the outer trenches. From 1930H, 19 February to 0730H, 20 February, seven USAF gunships and six flareships were employed in support of the Rangers. On several occasions during the night the gunships were directed by the ground commander to fire into the outer trenches. Then from 0730H to 1430H on 20 February, 32 sorties of USAF fighters struck the enemy positions. Helicopter resupply and medical evacuation were attempted under cover of tactical fighters, helicopter gunships and artillery; however, both of the first two helicopters to land were hit by mortar fire. One subsequently crashed and burned, the other succeeded in getting to FSB 30. Heavy mortar attacks continued through the afternoon. Communication with the Ranger commander was lost at 1820H and by 1900H the position was abandoned. One hundred and fifty Rangers exfiltrated to the 21st Ranger's position arriving at 2145H.[80/] The 39th Ranger Battalion was out of the battle having suffered 178 soldiers killed or missing and 145 wounded. Only 108 members were considered combat effective on 21 February.[81/] During its three-day struggle the 39th Rangers had fought the 102d NVA Regiment. Enemy losses were estimated at 639 KIA.[82/]

LULL IN THE FIGHTING

The enemy now divided his attention between the remaining Rangers and the 3d Airborne Battalion at FSB 31. Both positions received attacks by fire on 21 February. However, the attacks were infrequent and not followed by infantry.

On 22 February, thirteen helicopter sorties successfully evacuated 122 wounded Rangers from the 21st Ranger Battalion area. The Ranger LZ had been "prepped" for nearly two hours by tactical air strikes, helicopter gunships, ARA and artillery. None of the medevac "choppers" suffered a hit.[83/] Following the evacuation of the wounded, 400 soldiers remained at the 21st Ranger's position.

Elements of the 1st and 3d Infantry Regiments continued their southeasterly thrust reaching Routes 92D and 914 then moving northwest along these routes searching and destroying. One unit found the POL pipeline previously hit by gunships of the U.S. 2d Squadron, 17 Air Cavalry. The pipeline was destroyed at intervals over a five kilometer distance.[84/] These wide-ranging infantry units moved by helicopter back to the edge of the escarpment on 23 February, leaving only the 1st Battalion, 1st Infantry Regiment on the southern salient. It moved to a position four kilometers north of the intersection of Routes 92 and 914. The 4th Battalion, 3d Infantry Regiment made a combat assault into LZ Brown and the 3d Regiment headquarters was lifted with the 2d Battalion into FSB Delta I.[85/]

Weather and hostile fire on the pick-up zone delayed the movement of the 1st Infantry Division elements to the fire support bases along the escarpment. However, the 3d Regiment did succeed in lifting engineers and some artillery from FSB Hotel II to FSB Delta I.[86/]

LOGISTICAL SUPPORT AT KHE SANH

A massive resupply effort to sustain the U.S. and ARVN combat forces was mounted at the Khe Sanh combat support base. It was critically important that adequate stores of JP-4 fuel and ammunition of all types be maintained at Khe Sanh. The planned delivery of this cargo by C-130 aircraft was delayed until 15 February by the necessity to cover the assault landing strip with aluminum matting. Until 17 February when C-130 operations reached 40 sorties a day, all supplies had to be transported by Army trucks or CH-47 helicopters and U.S. Marine CH-53 helicopters. This strained the Army's transport capability and engineering force, which had to expend great effort keeping Route 9 passable. After the C-130 operations began, the POL and ammunition levels reached the desired reserve.

The ARVN forces were resupplied almost entirely by helicopter. The Armored Task Force and the Airborne units designated to secure Route 9 were never able to insure safe passage for ARVN truck convoys. Consequently, it was not a reliable means of resupply. 87/

The helicopter traffic about Khe Sanh caused difficulties for arriving and departing C-130 aircraft especially during the periods when only one runway was available. These difficulties were attributed to the extremely high density of rotary wing traffic, a lack of air discipline on the part of some U.S. Army helicopter pilots, and the low level of experience of Army tower operators in controlling the complex fixed wing and rotary wing air traffic situation at Khe Sanh. To correct this problem, an Air Force control tower and operators were provided by the 1st Mobile Communications Group at Clark to assist in this air traffic control problem. 88/

Despite the difficulties, however, the resupply effort was always adequate to sustain the combat units.

ARC LIGHT

The B-52 Arc Light strikes provided heavy fire power for the ARVN invasion force. By 23 February, 399 Arc Light sorties had been flown in support of Lam Son 719. The cumulative results to that date included 201 enemy killed plus 813 tons of ammunition, 400 structures and vast quantities of supplies and equipment destroyed.*[89/] The targets were selected by CG, I Corps, on the basis of visual and photo reconnaissance as well as other sources of intelligence and approved by MACV. The targets were heavy troop concentrations, bivouac areas, supply sites and bunker complexes.[90/] The ARVN command reported that B-52 strikes on 12 February had hit the Headquarters Command Post of the NVA 308th Division killing 35 and destroying communication equipment.[91/] On 18 February three Arc Light cells delivered their bomb loads on targets in the area of Routes 92 and 926, supporting the southerly thrust of the 1st Infantry Division. Arc Light sorties were targeted in the Ranger Hill area during the desperate battle of the 39th Rangers. The ARVN stated that these strikes "disrupted enemy operations" and killed an unspecified number of enemy soliders.[98/] More concrete reports of B-52 strike results came on 25 February from the 3d Battalion, 1st Infantry Regiment which searched two Arc Light areas. It found a total of 142 enemy dead, four tons of mortars and artillery ammunition destroyed, various pieces of military equipment and a large tunnel complex damaged.[93/] A tactic of using Arc Light against enemy troops in contact was employed by units of the 1st Infantry Division. They would designate a target area where enemy troops were known to be deployed, engage these troops in combat in this area prior to the Arc Light Time-Over-Target and then just before the TOT withdraw from the target area. For a single

---

*Actually the results of Arc Light strikes could not be accurately determined because tac air also struck many of the same targets.

such engagement by the 1st Battalion, 3d Infantry Regiment on 27 February, 29 enemy soldiers were killed by air.[94]

TACTICAL AIR

Tactical air strikes in the period 20-25 February were predominately directed at known enemy positions and storage areas in the daylight hours and to support troops in contact or to destroy trucks at night. More than 110 sorties per day were flown in direct support of ground forces in the Laos AO of Lam Son 719. Fully one-third of the sorties were against targets on the northern flank in support of the Rangers still engaged in screening operations. The balance of the sorties flew in the Airborne and Infantry AOs in numbers which varied each day. Because the Infantry had aggressively thrust at the enemy's LOCs to Base Area 611, they tended to have more daytime contact with the enemy and thus to employ more tactical air strikes, as well as Arc Lights, against enemy troops. For example, the 3d Battalion, 1st Infantry located an enemy force in bunkers at 0930H on 25 February. The infantrymen requested tactical fighter strikes on the positions which were made. A search of the area revealed 17 enemy soldiers killed by air action.[95]

ENEMY STRIKES HARD - OBJECTIVE 31

On 25 February the NVA forces launched a generalized offensive against the ARVN positions. It began with the pre-dawn attack on a 1st Airborne position near FSB A Loui. During this engagement the friendlies were supported by a FAC (O-2), a flareship (C-123) and a gunship (AC-130) and with fighter strikes employing all weather delivery techniques. The contact continued until dawn. The Rangers reported heavy vehicle traffic on Route 925 and noisy troop activity near their position. They requested a flareship. It was provided though the enemy was not sighted.[96/]

By 1100H, enemy attacks were in progress around the entire ARVN perimeter from the Rangers to the forward units of the 1st Infantry Division as well as behind the lines near FSB Alpha. The persistent incoming mortar fire on Hotel II forced cancellation of the 1st Infantry's plans to abandon the fire support base and move two battalions to LZ Brown. The division's positions south along Route 92 received repeated mortar barrages followed by infantry attacks. Thirty-two tactical air strikes supported the 1st Infantry Division in its resistance to the enemy pressure.[97/] An F-4 delivering napalm on enemy troops 10 kilometers northwest of Hotel II was hit by ground fire. The pilot was killed and the backseater executed a dual ejection after flying the aircraft back to Phu Cat.[98/]

The Rangers received heavy mortar fire followed by ground attack. The Rangers chose to evacuate their vulnerable position. They were lifted by helicopter to Objective 30 and one-half of them were carried on to Khe Sanh. The remaining 160 rangers joined with the 2d Airborne Battalion in the defense of Objective 30. This position received attacks throughout the day.[99/]

The most determined attack was made on Objective 31. The 3d Airborne Brigade Headquarters with the 3d Airborne Battalion, an artillery battery and a Ranger Reconnaissance Company occupied this post. Mortar fire began at 0700. A FAC searching for 12.7mm machine gun positions two kilometers northeast of the Airborne main camp sighted over 100 trenches and small-arms gunpits along the ridge line. After observing gun fire from these positions, he delivered two flights of F-4s against them. The strikes hit the enemy as he advanced to within 250 meters of the Airborne perimeter defenses.[100/] The ground commander reported that an entire enemy mortar platoon had been killed by the air strikes. However, Objective 31 was encircled by NVA troops. Mortar and artillery fire continued to rain on the base camp. Helicopter gunships and artillery sought to suppress the enemy fire between air strikes. At 1430H a FAC spotted three enemy tanks within 30 meters to the east of the airborne positions. It was a coordinated tank and infantry attack. The FAC directed tactical air strikes on the tanks. Four A-7s delivering 16 MK 83s, four MK 82s and four Rockeyes destroyed the three tanks and killed 30 enemy soldiers. Three more tanks were seen coming up the hill from Route 92B. They were hit by seven sets of fighters delivering primarily BLU-27 and MK 82. During these strikes one F-4 was downed but the tanks were destroyed and 100 NVA killed. However, the enemy pressed the attack with more tanks and troops. A thunderstorm broke over the battle area making it impossible to get fighters on to the enemy from 1540H to 1735H.[101/] During this time a tank and enemy infantry penetrated the defenses and occupied the north and northwest sides of the position forcing the ARVN troops to the southern edge. The battle raged into the night with USAF gunships, flareships and FACs providing continuous support. Fires from burning tanks dotted the hill. Communications were lost at 2330H when the artillery commander called for artillery directly on his position because the enemy was digging into the roof of his bunker.

By dawn the defenders had withdrawn to a position on the ridge south of Objective 31. The 3d Airborne Brigade commander and part of his staff were dead or missing. The enemy occupied Objective 31 with tanks and infantry. Tactical air strikes and helicopter gunships attacked the enemy tanks throughout the day of 26 February. One company of the 3d Airborne Battalion, moved south and linked up with an armored relief column pushing up from Route 92. The relief units were stopped by heavy enemy resistance several hundred meters short of FSB 31.[102/] (See Figure 10.)

On 25 February, 108 tactical air sorties were flown in support of the beleaguered airborne units. Five Arc Light cells (three B-52s each cell) delivered their massive bombloads around FSB 31 on 26 February. The 64th NVA Regiment with tank support had made a determined and briefly successful assault.[103/] But it paid a high price. The I Corps headquarters reported that 250 NVA soldiers were killed and 15 tanks (12 PT-76, three T-34) were destroyed.[104/]

The 1st Airborne Division was reorganized on 26 February when the 2d Airborne Brigade headquarters was lifted into the LZ near Objective 30 and assumed responsibility for the northeastern AO. The 11th Airborne Battalion followed the Brigade CP into the area on 27 February.

The 1st Infantry Division had a series of brisk contacts with the enemy on 26 and 27 February in which they had the full range of air support. In searches on 27 February, they found 227 enemy killed by tactical air or Air Light strikes.[105/] The KBA total mounted on 28 February when 1st

Infantry elements found 47 more bodies in areas hit by tactical air strikes. Airborne units on the same day found some 85 enemy bodies in Arc Light target zones near FSB 31. 106/

Enemy armor was sighted throughout the AO on 28 February. Tanks were seen both east and west of A Loui on Route 9 and south on Route 92C to a point west of LZ Don. 107/ Tactical air strikes were credited with destroying 15 tanks and damaging two others. 108/ At 0100H on 1 March eight enemy tanks were sighted on Route 9 eight kilometers west of A Loui moving southeast. They were observed, engaged and dispersed by a FAC and AC-130 gunship. 109/ U.S. Air Cavalry units continued to report numerous tank sightings on 1 and 2 March; however, most of the tanks were stationary and heavily camouflaged. Many of the tanks were using huts for concealment. The pilots reported that most of the tanks appeared to be medium rather than light tanks. 110/ (See Figure 11.)

The 1st Infantry Division continued to be in contact with the enemy on its searching operations. However, enemy-initiated activity slackened noticeably, permitting the extraction and redeployment of three battalions of the 3d Regiment. 111/ During this period of relative quiet, the division resupplied its battalions by helicopter and evacuated its wounded.

At 1850H on 1 March the 17th Armored Cavalry Squadron and 3d Airborne Battalion in the vicinity of FSB 31 were hit with a coordinated tank and infantry attack by a regimental-size force. Artillery, tactical air strikes, gunships and flareships supported the friendly troops until the enemy broke off the attack. This fight resulted in killing 250 enemy soldiers and

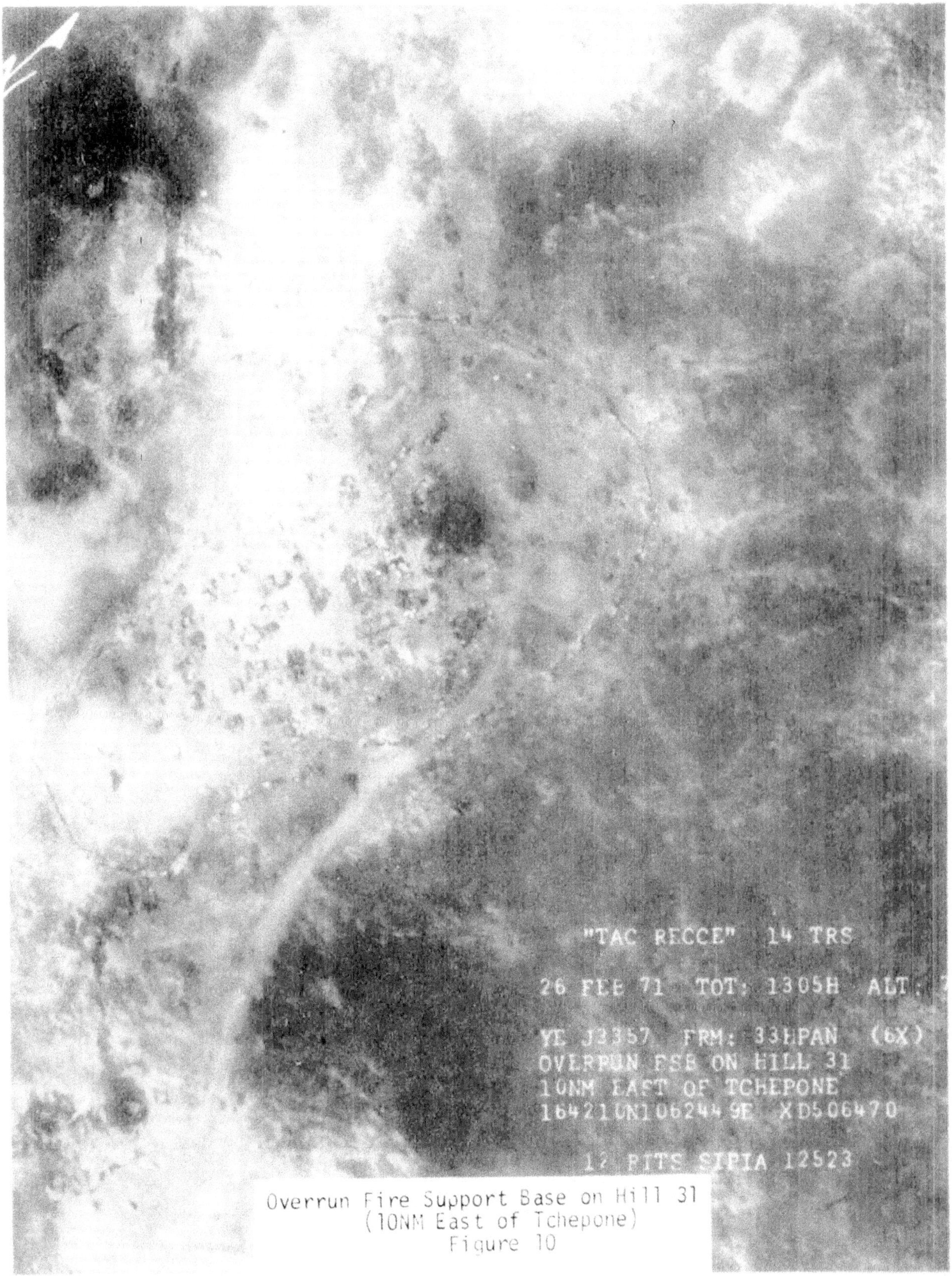

"TAC RECCE" 14 TRS

26 FEB 71 TOT: 1305H ALT.

YE J3357 FRM: 33HPAN (6X)
OVERRUN FSB ON HILL 31
10NM EAST OF TCHEPONE
164210N1062449E XD506470

12 PITS SIPIA 12523

Overrun Fire Support Base on Hill 31
(10NM East of Tchepone)
Figure 10

Destroyed PT-76 Tank
(1.5KM Northeast of Hill 31)
FIGURE 11

destroying 15 enemy tanks. The ARVN suffered eight soldiers killed, 50 wounded and six Armored Personnel Carriers damaged.112/

During the night of 1-2 March, the 2d Airborne Battalion at FSB 30 received mortar and rocket fire of increasing intensity. At 1530H on 2 March, the attack-by-fire was followed by a tank-supported infantry charge. Intense fighting continued till 2100H when a lull occurred. Thirty-six tactical air sorties hit the enemy surrounding FSB 30 during the daylight hours. AC-119 and AC-130 gunships and C-123 flareships were on station all night over the site. Heavy fighting broke out again about 0300H on 3 March and continued into the daylight hours when tactical air and Arc Light sorties struck the enemy positions.113/ The ground attack lasted ten hours with the ARVN claiming 98 enemy killed while losing one ARVN soldier killed and three wounded.114/

The locus of intense close fighting shifted back to the 17th ACS and 8th Airborne at FSB 31* on the night of 3 March. With the dawn the ARVN counted 383 enemy dead and two captured.115/

It is apparent that the widespread offensive conducted by the NVA 70B Corps from 25 February to 3 March was designed to halt the ARVN advance, inflict heavy casualties and force a withdrawal. Troop and supply build-up had occurred along Routes 1032 and 925 on the north and 914 and 926 in the south prior to launching the offensive. It was a very "conventional"

---

*The terms FSB 31, Objective 31 and Hill 31 all refer to the same geographic position.

series of battles. Tanks and infantry assaulted fixed artillery positions. The assaults were met, though not always stopped, by air-delivered firepower.

The ARVN forces had held against the enemy offensive and on 3 March the 1st Infantry Division resumed its western drive.

RAID TO TCHEPONE

During the first three days of March, I Corps positioned additional forces in the Khe Sanh area for introduction into Laos. These forces included the 7th Armored Cavalry Squadron, the 2d Infantry Regiment and the 258th Vietnamese Marine Brigade. With the reinforcements and a series of rapid heliborne assaults, the ARVN regained the initiative.

LZ LO LO

The 3d Battalion, 1st Infantry Regiment made a combat assault into LZ Lo Lo on 3 March beginning at 1000H. The assault was interrupted twice by intense hostile fire on the troop-lift helicopters. Forty-two helicopters were hit, 20 were declared nonflyable and seven were destroyed. Tactical air strikes were called in to suppress the ground fire and the assault was completed at 1615H. [116/] (For a full discussion of the LZ preparation see Chapter IV.) The 3d Battalion secured the area surrounding the LZ and constructed a fire support base. At 0800H on 4 March while searching in the vicinity of LZ Lo Lo the infantrymen engaged an enemy force killing 83 of them and capturing more than 40 weapons. [117/]

The 2d Battalion, 1st Infantry Regiment, was helilifted into Lo Lo at 1150H on 4 March. It was followed by lifts of artillery, ammunition, supplies and the 4th Battalion completing the build-up of Lo Lo at 1640H.

LZ LIZ

The 1st Battalion, 1st Infantry Regiment made a heliborne combat assault into LZ Liz at 1735H on 4 March. Sixty-five lift helicopters were required. Eighteen helicopters were hit, two of them were destroyed while 16 were recovered.[118/] Again enemy gunners had inflicted heavy damage on the U.S. Army helicopter forces even though sixty-one tactical air strikes were used in the LZ preparation. (See Chapter IV.)

The 1st Battalion dug in and constructed a fire support base on the high ground adjacent to the LZ.

MARINES REPLACE THE 1ST INFANTRY

While the 1st Infantry Regiment moved west establishing new fire bases on the rim of the escarpment, their place in the line on the southern flank was taken by Marine units. The 7th Battalion, 258th VNMC Brigade had been inserted at FSB Delta on 2 March and was joined by the 2d and 4th Battalions, 147th VNMC Brigade on 4 March. The next day the 8th Battalion, 147th VNMC Brigade closed to FSB Delta by air. The Marines now were responsible for the security of the eastern portion of the AO south of Route 9.[119/]

LZ SOPHIA

The advance west continued on 5 March when the 4th and 5th Battalions of the 2d Infantry Regiment were helilifted from Khe Sanh to LZ Sophia.

The assault was completed at 1640H. While the 4th Battalion set about emplacing the artillery pieces and constructing defenses, the 5th Battalion pushed out and searched the surrounding area. They found a former enemy camp destroyed by air strikes. There were 124 enemy dead, 33 huts damaged plus 71 weapons, eight tons of rice and 55 blocks of TNT found.[120]

LZ HOPE

The 2d and 3d Battalion, 2d Infantry Regiment were delivered by helicopter into LZ Hope from Khe Sanh on 6 March. The first helicopter set down on the landing zone at 1206H and the two battalion lift of 60 helicopters was complete at 1343H. Only one aircraft took a hit on the assault. (See Chapter IV.)

The infantry moved off the LZ to high ground. In searching operations they discovered 102 enemy killed by air, along with five trucks, six 12.7mm machine guns, 225 gallons of POL in drums and assorted small arms. Elements of the 2d Battalion then moved southwest towards the town of Tchepone.[121]

SEARCH AND DESTROY

Throughout the area of operations the ARVN forces searched in the vicinity of the fire support bases and engaged the enemy in small unit actions. They continued to find evidence of "substantial enemy equipment and personnel losses as a result of tac air and Arc Light strikes."[122] The 3d Infantry Regiment command post at FSB Lo Lo received an attack-by-fire followed by enemy infantry. The enemy force was repulsed with 31 killed. Several Airborne units received mortar attacks with little damage sustained.[123]

The 3d Battalion VNMC was introduced to FSB Hotel along with the 9th Battalion, 369th Marine Brigade. Six Marine battalions were now in Laos. South Vietnamese strength in Laos reached 16,844 with 18 battalions of infantry (including Airborne), four artillery battalions, three armored cavalry squadrons, two engineer battalions and six Marine battalions. All Rangers were removed from Laos and conducted their operations in the remainder of the campaign from the 1st Ranger Group headquarters at FSB Phu Loc.[124]

HIGH WATER MARK - TCHEPONE

The invasion reached its high water mark on 7 March when three battalions of the 2d Infantry Regiment conducted operations in and about the town of Tchepone. The 2d Battalion searched in and north of the former town site. The Third Battalion searched southeast of the town on the north bank of the Xe Pon River. The 4th Battalion had moved northwest from FSB Sophia and searched on the south bank of the river. The 5th Battalion remained in the vicinity of FSB Sophia.[125]

The 2d Battalion reported finding 1220 122mm rockets destroyed by an Arc Light strike at 1300H and observed 500 secondary explosions, two kilometers northeast of Tchepone, following an Arc Light Strike at 1430H. FACs reported observing over 1600 secondary explosions from the same area on 8 March after a tactical air strike. One kilometer south of this point, the 2d Battalion discovered 52 dead bodies and a cache of stored weapons on 8 March.[126]

Resupply missions were flown to all fire support bases on 7 and 8 March. Contact with the enemy was light except at FSBs Lo Lo and Delta. Both of these sites experienced mortar and rocket attacks followed by multi-company assaults.[127/]

Saturation search operations continued on 9 March by all units of the 1st Infantry Division. A total of 59 enemy bodies and numerous destroyed supply caches were found in areas hit by tactical air strikes. The 1st Infantry Regiment observed enemy tanks near its command post. The tanks were hit by 155mm and 175mm artillery resulting in three tanks destroyed and five left burning. The 4th Battalion of this regiment engaged an enemy force south of the Xe Pon River killing twelve Communist soldiers.[128/]

Ground searches on 10 March confirmed more enemy killed by Arc Light strikes. Six kilometers southeast of Sophia, 391 bodies were found, 144 were counted in the 1st Infantry Regiment area, 150 near FSB 30 and 60 just north of FSB Delta.[129/]

All three battalions that had been searching in the Tchepone area withdrew on 10 March to the escarpment and deployed to the east and south towards the high ground above Route 914.[130/]

ENEMY BUILD-UP

At 1230H on 10 March FSB Sophia received 122 rounds of mixed 82mm and 122mm mortar rounds. Twelve ARVN soldiers were wounded and six 105mm howitzers were damaged.[131/] Though enemy resistance to the Tchepone raid had been very light, there was reason to believe that the NVA was preparing

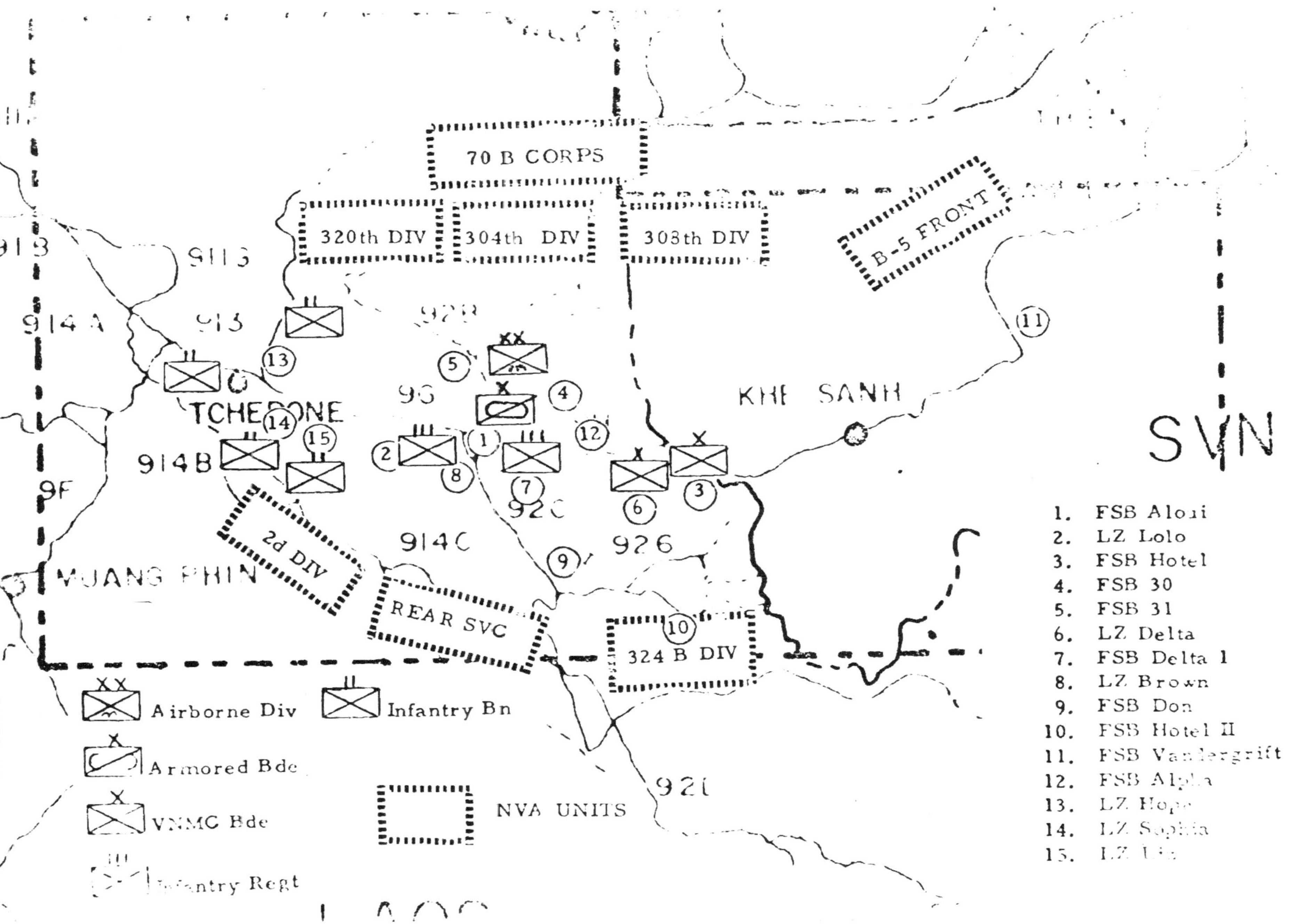

1. FSB Aloni
2. LZ Lolo
3. FSB Hotel
4. FSB 30
5. FSB 31
6. LZ Delta
7. FSB Delta 1
8. LZ Brown
9. FSB Don
10. FSB Hotel II
11. FSB Vandergrift
12. FSB Alpha
13. LZ Hope
14. LZ Sophia
15. LZ Liz

FIGURE 12

for another offensive. Sensor detections showed heavy traffic on all routes coming into the battle area during the week of 3-10 March. Traffic on Routes 1032B, 914B and 92A was especially heavy.132/ Ten southbound tracked vehicles were detected moving along Route 914B south of FSB Liz. Likewise, southbound tracked vehicles were detected in the Ban Raving entry area.133/

The 70B Corps and attached units had suffered approximately 12,000 casualties (including over 3,000 KBA) since the Lam Son operation began. These losses were apparently replaced by the introduction of five more regiments into the war zone. Combat troop strength rose to more than 24,000 organized in some twelve infantry regiments, two artillery regiments and one tank regiment. Additionally, there were 11,000 rear service troops in the area. The forces were approximately evenly divided in their deployment north and south of the ARVN position.134/ With its units replenished and reinforced, the NVA command waited for the opportunity to mount a heavy attack against the South Vietnamese in Laos.

RETURN TO THE EAST

The Tchepone raiders (2d Infantry Regiment) continued their easterly deployment on 11 March. The 2d Regiment headquarters, the 2d and 5th Battalions and a 105mm artillery battery were helilifted from LZ Liz to LZ Brown "leapfrogging" over the 1st Regiment at Lo Lo into the center of the 1st Infantry Division's positions on the escarpment. The 4th Battalion operated around FSB Sophia and the 3d Battalion secured LZ Liz.135/

On 12 March, the 2d Regiment and its accompanying two battalions established a new fire support base at Sophia East (one kilometer west of LZ Brown). The 3d Battalion was lifted out of LZ Liz and arrived at LZ Moon (adjacent to FSB Sophia East) at 1708H. Immediately after this lift, the 4th Battalion was extracted from FSB Sophia and closed on LZ Moon at 1835H.[136/] The 2d Regiment consolidated its position and prepared for an attack south to interdict Route 914 at Cua Viet and Cua Tang.[137/]

The 4th Armored Battalion (Composite) joined the ARVN forces in Laos on 13 March. Its 260 personnel in 30 M41 tanks, nine M113 armored personnel carriers and two M548 light tracked recovery vehicles moved along Route 9 to FSB Alpha to augment route security operations. South Vietnamese strength in the Laotian AO reached its peak of 17,104 on this date.[138/]

The 1st Infantry Division continued its searching operation and redeployment maneuvers. The 2d Regiment command post moved by air to FSB Delta I. The 1st Regiment received three mortar and artillery attacks of increasing intensity on FSB Lo Lo and vicinity. These attacks-by-fire proved to be the prelude to four days of bitter fighting.

WITHDRAWAL FROM LAOS

The orderly, phased redeployment east along the escarpment with thrusts south to Route 914 which began on 10 March had met only token enemy resistance. The 2d Battalion, 2d Infantry Regiment, probing south on 14 March reached the edge of the high ground overlooking Route 914 and established a position two kilometers north of the road and conducted small unit probes down to it.[139/] Elements of the 2d Regiment reported that tactical air strikes destroyed two PT-76 tanks and an ammunition cache one kilometer east of LZ

Brown. Later they reported a battalion size enemy force two kilometers west of the tank site but adverse weather prevented tactical air strikes on the position.[140/] On the same day a FAC reported observing six enemy tanks 15 kilometers west of FSB A Loui on Route 9. The tanks were engaged and destroyed by tactical air.[141/] It was clear that the enemy had timed his offensive maneuvers to strike the ARVN forces in the most vulnerable phase of their operations, the withdrawal.

LO LO ABANDONED

From 0600H on 14 March until 1100H on 17 March, the 1st Infantry Regiment was in almost continuous heavy contact with enemy troops. FSB Lo Lo received mortar, rocket and 155mm artillery fire throughout 14 and 15 March. Resupply helicopters were unable to land at Lo Lo because of the intense ground fire. At 2200H on the night of 15 March the 3d Battalion and the 1st Infantry Regiment command post abandoned Lo Lo and moved to the high ground two kilometers east of the LZ. Four 155mm howitzers were destroyed in place prior to the evacuation. Four 105mm howitzers and one 155mm howitzer had been heavily damaged by enemy fire.[142/] Before the 1st Regiment withdrew, a high price was exacted from the attacking enemy. The enemy infantry sought to get as close as possible to the friendly positions to avoid U.S. air strikes. However, the 1st Regiment's commander called for B-52 strikes within 500 yards of his position.[143/] The commander discontinued tactical air support the night of 17-18 March just before his withdrawal. The regiment continued to engage the enemy while moving north and east off the escarpment and preparing for helicopter extraction on 18 March.

In the three days of intense fighting around Lo Lo, NVA losses were put at 1100 killed while the 1st Regiment suffered 66 soldiers killed and 192 wounded. The 1st Regiment command post plus the 1st, 2d and 3d Battalions were extracted from Laos to Khe Sanh on 18 March completing the lift at 1230H.[144/] The 4th Battalion covered the Regiment's withdrawal and was in intermittent heavy contact with the enemy through the night and until its extraction on 18 March. Fifty infantrymen including the Commander and Executive Officer of this battalion were killed and 80 wounded. But the 4th Battalion with air support killed 567 enemy soldiers.[145/] The 4th Battalion closed Khe Sanh by air at 1644H, 18 March.

THE RAIDERS ARE BLOODIED

Initially during this four-day battle of the 1st Infantry Regiment, the 2d Regiment had continued its searching and destroying operations. It called in numerous air strikes on base camps, supply caches, and enemy troop concentrations. In its searches from 14 to 17 March, its units found literally hundreds of enemy bodies obviously killed by air strikes.[146/] However, enemy pressure on the 2d Regiment mounted and its 2d Battalion which had been operating near Route 914 moved north to join the battalions operating in the FSB Sophia East and LZ Brown areas. The 2d Regiment CP had moved to FSB Delta I several days earlier. By 1000H, 17 March all four 2d Regiment battalions were on the high ground immediately south of LZ Brown and moving east toward FSB Delta I. The 5th Battalion which remained in the LZ Brown area to screen the withdrawal, reported that 80 enemy were killed by tactical air strikes during an engagement.[147/] The 5th Battalion was extracted by helicopter to Khe Sanh on 18 March completing the lift at 1545H.[148]/ The other three battalions moved off the escarpment during the night of 18-19 March. Large, well-coordinated, main force NVA units were now conducting heavy attacks on the infantrymen. These forces had flame throwers and heavy artillery. Rear service units moved with them employing antiaircraft artillery, thereby making resupply of the fire support bases not feasible. Thirty-two tactical air strikes were flown in support of the 2d Regiment in addition to U.S. Army gunship and artillery support. U.S. Air Force gunships and flareships covered the units throughout the night of 19 March as they moved towards FSB Delta I. The 2d Battalion claimed 85 enemy killed in the day's battle, the 3d Battalion reported 87 enemy killed and the 4th Battalion reported killing 195 Communist soldiers.[149]/ As they fought their way toward FSB Delta I, that position was receiving such intense mortar and artillery fire that only one of 26 requested helicopter resupply sorties landed on 19 March. Artillery pieces and ammunition dumps were destroyed by enemy fire. The position could not be held if it could not be resupplied. The 3d Battalion was extracted by helicopter from a pick-up zone four kilometers west of FSB Delta I, but 28 of the 40 helicopters in the lift received hits and were rendered nonflyable.[150]/ The intense antiaircraft fire forced the termination of efforts to extract the remaining two battalions on 20 March. The remainder of the 2d Regiment moved out to find more suitable pick-up zones. They were finally extracted on 21 March and closed Khe Sanh at 1830H exhausted and bloodied.[151]/

HASTENED WITHDRAWAL

Beginning on 18 March every ARVN position was hit by mortar, rocket and artillery fire. The airborne battalions on the northern flank received these attacks both day and night. Helicopter extraction of the most exposed unit, the 2d Airborne Battalion was attempted on 19 March but was cancelled after three tries because of very heavy ground fire on the LZ. The 2d and 7th Airborne Battalions remained in heavy contact with the enemy on the northern flank while the 1st Airborne Brigade and the Armored Task Force evacuated FSB A Loui. The 2d and 7th Battalions were extracted on 20 March completing the lift to Khe Sanh at 1815H. Both battalions were lifted on to Dong Ha closing at 1930H.[152/]

EVACUATION FROM A LOUI

The 1st Airborne Brigade and the Armored Task Force (11ACS, 17ACS, 8ABN and 9ABN) began the withdrawal from FSB A Loui at first light on 19 March. By 0730H the last elements of the column observed four enemy tanks moving towards A Loui and about one kilometer away from the site at that time. The tanks were stopped by artillery fire and subsequently destroyed by tactical air strikes at 0950H.[153/] The task force then proceeded east on Route 9 toward FSB Alpha. Four kilometers east of A Loui the end of the column was ambushed even though airborne troops were reportedly protecting the flanks. Rocket propelled grenade fire disabled one or more vehicles blocking the road. The column had included four disabled tanks, three disabled armored personnel carriers and three howitzers that were being towed. In the confusion that developed during the ambush, these vehicles and others were abandoned. Though tactical fighters and helicopter gunships were available, neither was requested by the task force commander. Later the commander requested air strikes on the vehicles which had been abandoned in order to prevent their use by the enemy. Tactical air strikes destroyed 18 vehicles.[154/] The armored column reached FSB Alpha and remained there overnight. The 4th Armored Battalion (Composite) and the 11th Airborne Battalion joined the column on 21 March as it proceeded east. Helicopters lifted seven 105mm howitzers, four 155mm howitzers, one 3/4 and one 2/1.2 ton truck from FSB Alpha to Khe Sanh on 20 March and the 1st Airborne Brigade CP, 5th Airborne Battalion and personnel of two artillery batteries on 21 March. With the departure of the armored column FSB Alpha was closed.[155/]

ALL UNITS IN CONTACT

All South Vietnamese units were under attack by enemy forces on 20 March. The Marines holding the southern flank at FSBs Delta and Hotel were under such heavy indirect artillery fire that the helicopters could not effect resupply. Delta was under heavier attack than Hotel. To break it, eight Arc Light strikes were put in around the Delta perimeter, three on the south, two on the east and three on the west. Contact was temporarily broken.[156/]

The NVA 324B Division with at least two regiments, the 29th and 803d, attempted to smash the Marines and cut off the ARVN withdrawal down Route 9. However, the Marines held and inflicted heavy losses on the NVA. The 147th

VNMC Brigade at FSB Delta reported that during the period from 1800H 19 March to 0600H 22 March, 1000 enemy soldiers were killed (400 by air strikes) and five captured while 85 Marines were killed and 238 wounded.157/

ARMOR IN TROUBLE

The Armored Task Force with its attached airborne units made its way toward FSB Bravo on 21 March. The column was attacked by a two-battalion-size enemy force at 1130H five kilometers west of the RVN-Laos border. The 7th and 11th Armored Cavalry Squadrons and the 8th Airborne Battalion were engaged by the attackers. The 6th Airborne Battalion joined in the battle which raged for seven hours. Tactical air strikes, helicopter gunships and U.S. artillery supported the ARVN units throughout the day. When contact was broken at 1830H, 32 ARVN soldiers had died, 135 were wounded and the destroyed vehicles included ten M41 tanks and 13 M113 armored personnel carriers. Faced with a road littered with damaged and destroyed vehicles, a culvert washed out and the threat of more ambushes, the Armored Task Force Commander chose to turn his column of 100 vehicles from the road and take an alternate route to the border. The task force and its airborne screen spent the night near FSB Bravo. The enemy harassed the force intermittently during the night but the contacts were not serious. Three AC-130 gunships were employed with FACs and flareships throughout the night, to aid in fending off the attackers.158/ In the morning the column reached the Xe Pon River but was unable to find a suitable ford. Bulldozers and engineering equipment, as well as POL, were delivered by helicopter on 22 March to facilitate the river crossing. To protect the column while it was stopped at the edge of the river, five airborne companies were deployed north of Route 9 towards the border and the 9th and 11th Airborne Battalions moved across the river and established positions to the east of it.[159/]

At 1430H a FAC reported sighting an estimated 20 enemy tanks located eight kilometers west of the rear of the ARVN column. Five minutes later a second FAC confirmed nine enemy tanks moving east on Route 9 at about 30 miles per hour. He requested tactical fighters and shortly thereafter a pair of F-100s engaged the lead tank, then only five kilometers from the friendly armored task force. The fighters were equipped with close air support ordnance "snake and nape" (MK 82, 500 pound, high drag bomb; and BLU-27, napalm). This initial set of F-100s delivered its ordnance on two T-54 tanks without results. The second set of F-100s came on station and the FAC directed them on to the lead tank, a T-54. The number one fighter missed the tank on his first pass and the number two F-100 took heavy automatic weapons fire and crashed. The lead F-100 made a second pass, destroying the tank with a direct hit. This attack was immediately followed by another flight of F-100s that destroyed a second T-54. The third T-54 hit a land mine and was immobilized. It was then struck by an F-100 flight and destroyed.[160/] The rest of the tanks (PT-76s) dispersed and headed for cover. However, two PT-76 tanks were destroyed by an F-4 flight before reaching a safe haven. The threat to the retreating ARVN column had been temporarily thwarted.

The Armored Task Force continued its engineering efforts to prepare a crossing site at the Xe Pon River. However, the site was not ready at nightfall so the column of vehicles remained on the west bank of the river through the night. There was no contact with the enemy during the hours of darkness. At 0630H on 23 March, all the vehicles had crossed the river and were rolling east to the border. Link-up of the Armored Task Force with elements of the U.S. 1st Brigade, 5th Infantry (Mech) took place at 0915H. The ARVN 1st Armored Brigade crossed back into the Republic of Vietnam 43 days after it had left with only 89 vehicles (22 M41 tanks, 54 M113 armored personnel carriers, seven M-106 water trailers, two M125 heavy cargo trucks, three M548 light recovery vehicles and one D-2 bulldozer).[161] But, it had evaded with the help of tactical air the disaster planned for it by the Communists. From 19 March to 23 March, tactical air strikes destroyed or severely damaged 30 enemy tanks.

The 1st Airborne Division and the 1st Armored Brigade were home again. The 1st Ranger Group and 1st Infantry Division were already out thus, only the six battalions of Marines and the stragglers remained in Laos. As the ARVN units returned to Quang Tri Province (Lam Son East), they deployed to engage enemy forces in the Republic of Vietnam in the remaining days of Operation Lam Son 719.

ALL OUT BUT THE STRAGGLERS

While the Armored Task Force was wending its way towards the border, the 147th VNMC Brigade at FSB Delta was in a desperate fight against enemy tanks and infantry. Its three battalions with nine 105mm howitzers were surrounded by the enemy and in continuous contact from 21 through 23 March. Forty tactical air sorties were flown in a two-and-one-half-hour period (0725H-1006H) on 22 March.[162/] Poor visibility and low ceilings prevented any more sorties until midafternoon. Evening ground fire was too intense for helicopter resupply or medical evacuation. During the night of 22-23 March USAF flareships and gunships were on station over FSB Delta but did not fire because of uncertainty as to the Marine positions.[163/] In the early morning hours the brigade moved off FSB Delta to a position on the ridge three kilometers northeast of Delta. The Marines destroyed their remaining artillery at the fire support base before departing to find a suitable pick-up zone for helicopter extraction. From 1100H to 1300H 12 tactical air strikes struck FSB Delta to destroy the ammunition and kill enemy soldiers. Extraction of the 147th VNMC Brigade began at 1400H on 23 March but enemy antiaircraft fire became too heavy by 1453H to continue the lift. Four hundred thirty Marines (of whom 200 were wounded) had been extracted by the time the lift was suspended.[164/] The remainder of the brigade moved east towards FSB Hotel to join with the 258th VNMC Brigade defending that position. Both brigades were helilifted out from FSB Hotel on 24 March. All units were out of Laos by 1735H.[165/]

The 44 days of fighting cost the South Vietnamese 1118 killed, 4081 wounded and 209 missing. The ARVN estimate of the enemy's losses show 13,341 killed (4126 killed by air) and 51 captured. More than 8,000 tactical air strikes were flown by all the air services involved in the campaign.[166/] The campaign was a stringent test by fire of the South Vietnamese fighting ability, helicopter mobility in the battle zone and USAF striking power in close air support of ground forces.

LAM SON EAST

The U.S. Forces in Quang Tri Province who protected the allied LOC and provided the logistical support for the Vietnamese troops in Laos had a very busy 44 days. The Communist B5 Front made a concerted effort to disrupt the flow of supplies and equipment down Route 9. The difficulties in constructing and maintaining landing strips at Khe Sanh for the C-130s forced the U.S. Army to transport more of the material by truck convoy than had been planned. These convoys were lucrative targets for enemy ambushes. These ambushes occurred on a daily basis despite the efforts of the mobile combat teams fielded by the 1st Brigade, 5th Infantry to screen the route.

Every combat support base (Dong Ha, Quang Tri, Khe Sanh and Da Nang) and all the fire support bases received mortar, rocket and sapper attacks. The frequency and severity of these attacks appear to have coincided with the ebb and flow of the NVA offensives in Lam Son West (Laos). The most severe attacks were directed at Khe Sanh. It received daily mortar and rocket attacks beginning on 19 March. Four attacks by fire, including 59 rounds of 122mm artillery, hit Khe Sanh on 21 March killing two U.S. soldiers, destroying the primary control tower and damaging the landing strips sufficiently to close the field. A sapper attack made under cover of an artillery barrage on 22 March killed three Americans and wounded 13. Two helicopters were destroyed and four damaged. Several truckloads of ammunition were destroyed also.[168/] But all attacks were repulsed and the supplies never stopped moving.

The U.S. forces were augmented by units of the 23d Infantry Division and additional aviation assets as the campaign progressed. A large enemy build-up in the DMZ area threatened an invasion and allied forces prepared to meet it. However, the invasion never came.

The Air Force flew 1905 airlift sorties into Lam Son East carrying 12,846 passengers and 19,900 short tons of cargo. More than 1,000 tactical air strikes and 62 B-52 sorties were flown in support of the U.S. security forces. In addition, a variety of special missions was flown including photo reconnaissance, Commando Vault drops, psychological warfare leaflet drops and search and rescue missions.

For all of the operations associated with Lam Son 719, 137 Americans were killed, 818 were wounded and 42 were declared missing in action.

CHAPTER IV

AIR SUPPORT IN LAM SON 719

That the RVNAF could not have undertaken Lam Son 719 without air support has been established. Air made maneuverability possible, knocked out tanks, suppressed AA, and accounted for more than 4000 enemy casualties confirmed by ground units. This chapter examines various issues involved in providing air support for Lam Son 719.

PLANNING AIR SUPPORT

Sortie Allocations

In planning the tactical air support for Lam Son 719, 7AF decided that the ground force support sorties required would be filled by converting Steel Tiger interdiction sorties to the ground force support role.[*] Prior to Lam Son 719, ground force support sorties in Steel Tiger averaged only about ten percent of the total allocated to that area of Laos. These ground force support sorties for the most part were flown in support of Lao guerrilla operations against the Ho Chi Minh Trail. During Lam Son 719, however, the RVN employed elements of three divisions in the operations, and at the height of the action there were about 17,000 RVN troops engaged with the enemy. This heavy ground effort necessitated a large shift in the type of mission to which sorties were allocated in Steel Tiger. Figure 13 shows how the emphasis shifted from interdiction to ground force support

---

[*]These sorties in support of ground forces were primarily close air support sorties for troops in contact; but they also included sorties used for interdiction within the battlefield, for fire suppression and for landing zone preparation.

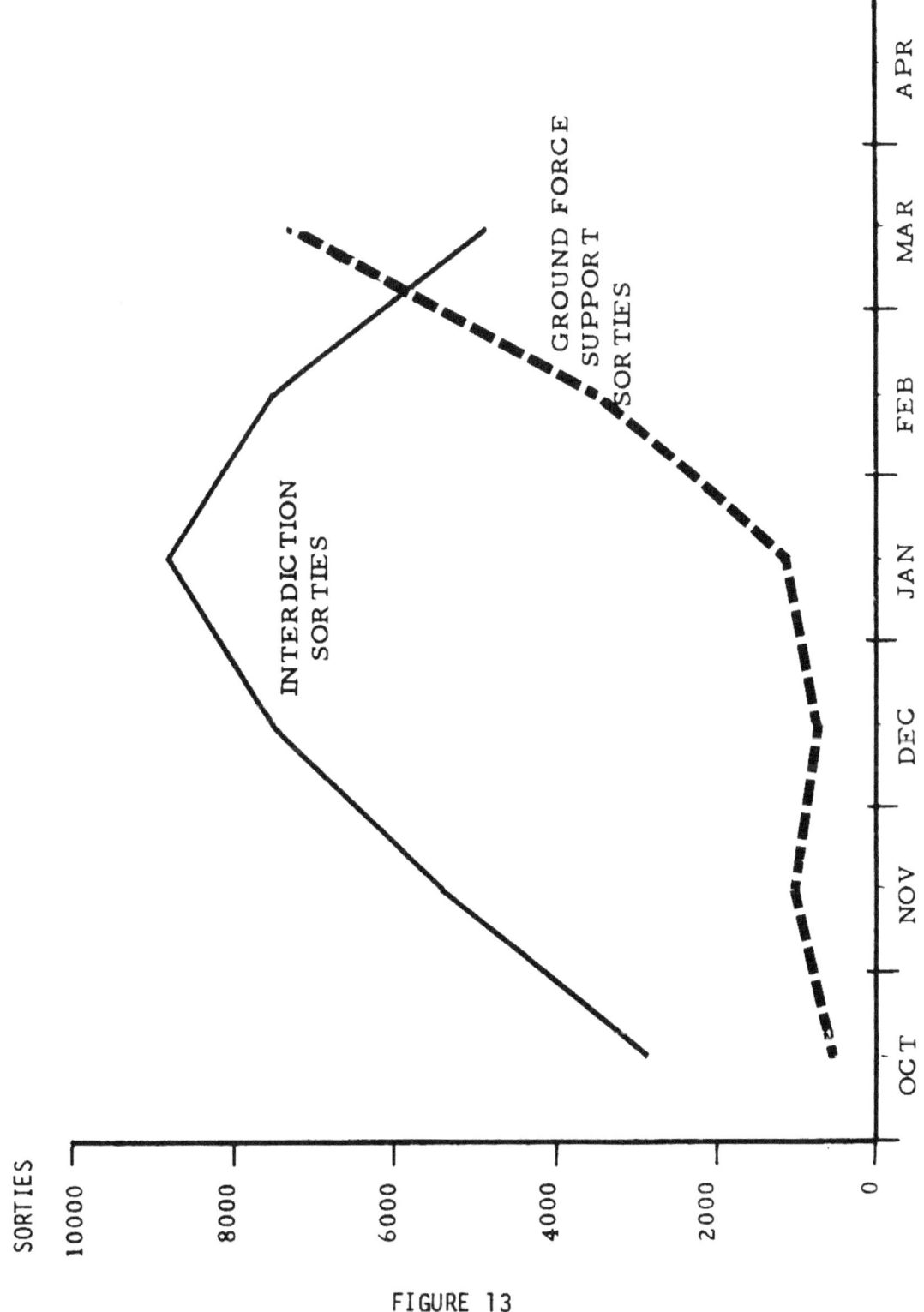

FIGURE 13

with the start of Lam Son 719 in February. This emphasis on ground force support rose steadily during the period of this report.[169]

During the early stages of the operation, the Lam Son 719 sorties were easily met from the sorties normally marked for Steel Tiger. However, as the operation progressed and the demands on tactical air became greater, it was necessary to increase the number of sorties provided for Lam Son 719. These additional commitments were met when 7AF directed that operational units increase their sortie rates. The rate was surged from 1.0 to a high on occasion of 2.0 for certain units and averaged about 1.3.

Throughout the operation, even during the peak surges for Lam Son 719, 7AF was able to maintain required daily sortie allocations for other areas of interest such as Barrel Roll (Northern Laos), Cambodia and the Republic of Vietnam. In northern Laos where a serious dry season threat existed against General Vang Pao's forces, approximately 40 sorties per day were made available to supplement the 70 provided by the Royal Laotian Air Force. In Cambodia, where ARVN forces were conducting a large operation (Toan Thang) centered on the Chup Plantation, some 50 U.S. strike sorties daily backed up those of the VNAF. In South Vietnam, the VNAF with approximately 70 sorties per day were picking up more than 50% of the total sortie load, but 7AF still provided an average of about 60 sorties per day. Figure 14 shows how the daily sortie allocations were distributed between Steel Tiger, Barrel Roll, Cambodia and the Republic of Vietnam, from 1 February through 8 April. Strike sorties for the Lam Son 719 part of Steel Tiger are shown only for the period covered by this report, 8 February through 24 March.

Security Aspects

Lam Son 719 planning was a very closely held secret. Only a few top officials within the military establishment had the details of the operation. At 7AF, as of 13 January, only the Commander, Vice Commander, the Deputy Chief of Staff for Operations and two other staff officers knew of the plan. At the field level, the only USAF officer with knowledge of the plan was the Deputy Director of I DASC at Da Nang. Within Army channels the situation was the same, and the plan for Lam Son 719 was closely held information at MACV Headquarters and at XXIV Corps.

These security precautions required that resources be assembled, subordinate units be alerted for operations, and personnel be deployed without individuals on the operating level knowing why such actions were being taken. The necessary actions were all accomplished, but the unavoidable restricted flow of information did have some repercussions on planning. The Army, for example, reported cases where units were requested to provide certain resources but were reluctant to comply, because they had previously been told that they were to stand down awaiting withdrawal and they knew nothing of Lam Son 719. 170/

PROBLEMS ARISING FROM VIETNAMESE CONTROL

Command Structure

It has already been noted that problems arose because of the complete RVN control of the ground operations in Laos. General Lam had absolute

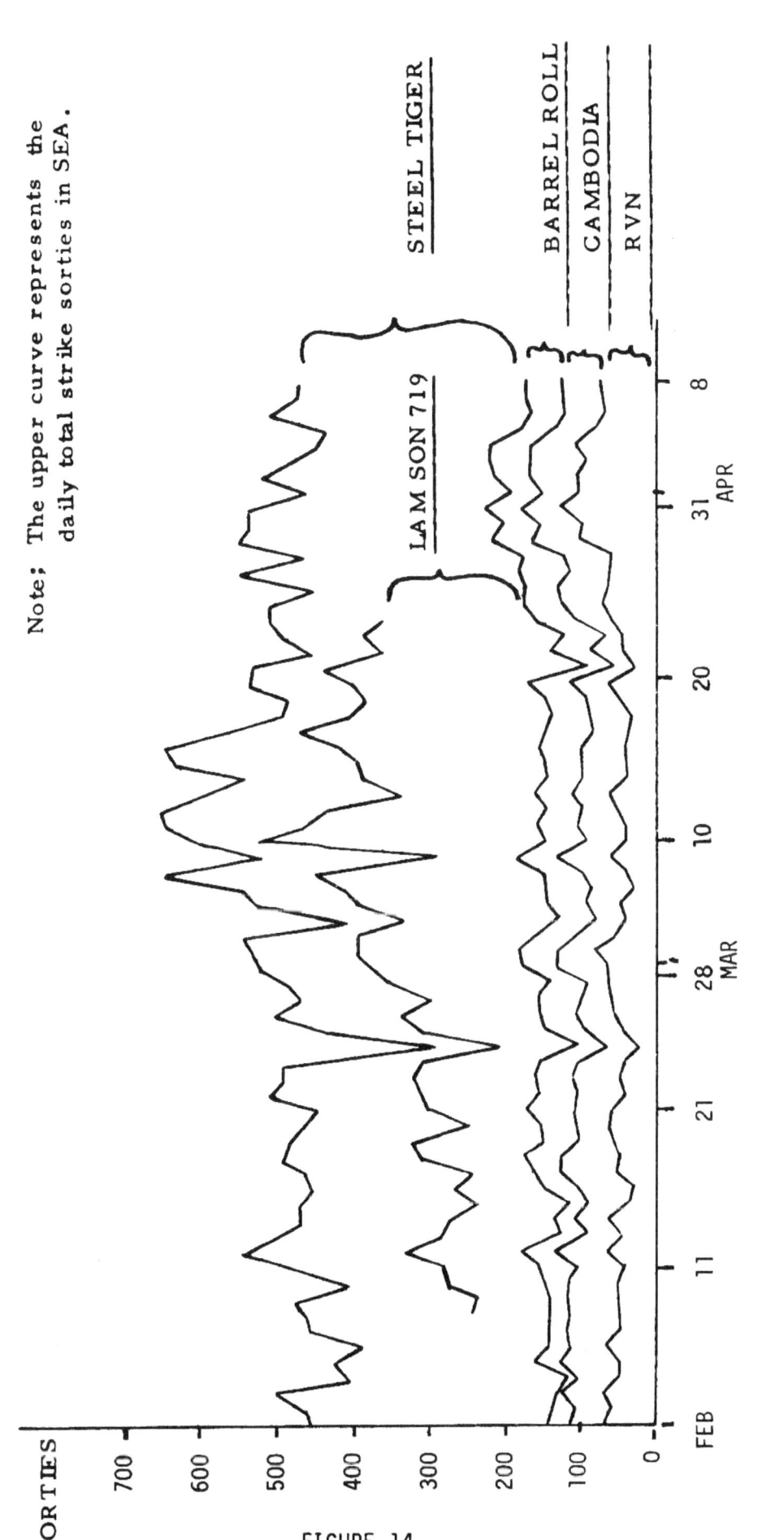

FIGURE 14

authority on the battlefield. Early in the campaign he frequently undertook heliborne operations supported by XXIV Corps but failed to coordinate such moves with 7AF representatives. Without such coordination, proper air support could not be provided.[171/] It also became clear early in the operation that I Corps tactical decisions were being made as the result of consultations between General Lam and President Nguyen Van Thieu, the only one to whose orders General Lam responded. This command structure was graphically illustrated in that major decision made on 12 February when the RVNAF were stalled at A Loui. After General Lam and President Thieu conferred on that date, it was announced that I Corps would not attempt to move rapidly to Tchepone at that time as originally planned. Rather, I Corps was to concentrate on destroying caches that they could uncover to the north and south of their position.[172/]

The battlefield decisions which General Lam made as Commander of I Corps and the plans which I Corps adopted as a result of consultations between President Thieu and General Lam were certainly the prerogative of the RVN. Nevertheless, such moves did create problems for the U.S. supporting forces. Frequently XXIV Corps and 7AF did not know what the battle plan for I Corps was, but such information was essential if the best possible support was to be provided. This lack of information was another factor which led to the establishment in early March of the Coordinating Committee of general officers to work with I Corps.[173/]

Language Problems

With I Corps operating in Laos without U.S. advisors, language problems were unavoidable, especially for the FACs who were to direct strikes at the request of ARVN ground commanders. Vietnamese observers were assigned to fly on U.S. FAC aircraft to act as interpreters. The problem of communication was revealed in many Hammer Daily Intelligence Summaries. For example, on 20 February Hammer 86 had so much difficulty in trying to communicate with his backseat interpreter that he did not use him at all. Instead he worked directly with the Vietnamese on the ground who did an outstanding job directing air strikes. The ground commander reported that his position had "survived" because of the timely action of the FAC and the English-speaking communicator on the ground.[174/]
Frequently it was necessary for the FACs to terminate their radio transmissions and ask repeated pointed questions of the Vietnamese observer in order to determine the ground situation and the strikes requested.

Several factors contributed to this problem with the backseat interpreters. Some of them just were not proficient enough in English. More important, however, was the fact that the observers were unfamiliar with the OV-10 aircraft. They had come from VNAF O-1 aircraft and had no experience in a higher performance airplane. They had arrived at Quang Tri only three days before the start of the operation and had received only one or two familiarization rides in the OV-10. Many of them became air sick on the first rocket pass (a very natural reaction for someone unfamiliar with the OV-10), and when that happened they were of little use to the pilot for the remainder of the mission.[175/] The most efficient arrangement for directing strikes was when the ground unit had a fluent English-speaker available.

TACTICAL AIR CONTROL

The Tactical Air Control System in conjunction with the Joint Air Ground Operations System in South Vietnam has been refined over the years to a relatively uncomplicated, responsive airspace and air strike control system. This system, with I DASC at Da Nang as the controlling agency, was used for tactical air support of the Allied forces operating in Vietnam in the eastern portion of the overall Lam Son 719 area.

The minor modifications to the established tactical air control system for control of tactical air in Laos supporting Lam Son 719 have been discribed in Chapter II. However, it should be noted that the on-the-scene coordinating agency between tactical air and the ground combat forces was DASC Victor. This Direct Air Support Center had direct communication with the Seventh Air Force Command Post (Blue Chip) and the ABCCC. DASC Victor had operational control of the Hammer Forward Air Controllers (23 TASS, Augmented) located at Quang Tri who proved to be the focal point of air strike and air space control over the Laotian battlefield in Lam Son 719.[176/]

After operations in Laos began, the amount of tactical air was steadily increased. This increase was accomplished by reducing the time interval between sets of fighters in the streams of air which were provided to the Lam Son 719 AO in Laos. The interval was reduced from an original fifteen minutes between sets to ten minutes or less. As the South Vietnamese moved west and the area of operation in Laos expanded, the number of daytime FACs was increased to six which was the maximum number the small area of operations would allow. There was also the additional seventh FAC, noted previously, who flew along the northern and western edges of the AO to act as an artillery spotter, and on one day there were actually eight FACs airborne at the same time. At night there were always three FACs on station. [177]

Strike aircraft reported in to the dedicated ABCCC and received an immediate handoff to a FAC. If the handoff could not be immediately effected, the aircraft were sent to designated orbit points to hold at specific flight levels. During the periods of heavy ground action, the strikes were employed to strike immediate request targets while at other times they were directed against preplanned targets or targets of opportunity identified by the FACs.

During the campaign, confusion involving radio frequencies was not uncommon. A typical example occurred on 3 March when Hammer 21 received a report of troops in contact from Hammer Control but was unable to contact the friendlies on the frequencies given him or to contact U.S. Army helicopters operating a few hundred meters south of the friendly position. This problem delayed a strike by incoming fighters until Hammer 21 could straighten out the communication difficulties with Hammer Control, and when he finally did, the fighters had time for only one pass.[178/]

There were also problems with U.S. Army and VNAF helicopters whose proposed actions and flights were frequently unknown to the FACs, the fighters or to the ABCCC. Complicating the situation, the helicopters were often not on the same communications frequency as the FACs, and consequently it was difficult to clear an area before putting in a tactical air strike.[179/]

These few examples illustrate difficulties involved in conducting an operation of this type. As the operation progressed, however, problems that arose were resolved.

AIRMOBILE OPERATIONS

The employment of helicopters was critical in the scheme of maneuver of Lam Son 719. For the first time in the Indochina War helicopters were the basic mode of transportation for a multi-division force engaged in a corps-size offensive operation. Multi-battalion maneuvers were completely dependent upon helicopters for assault, resupply and extraction. This mode of operation exploited the advantages of initiative, mobility, flexibility, speed and surprise in the initial assaults but suffered the acute disadvantage of vulnerability to hostile ground fire when forced to operate into fixed landing zones over a prolonged period of time. The lack of a ground line of communication for the ARVN maneuver units as an alternative to the air LOC posed serious problems for the U.S. Army and U.S. Air Force in their support of the South Vietnamese operations. The impact of these problems on tactics and techniques requires closer examination.

The terrain in the Lam Son 719 operational area is generally mountainous with dense vegetation. In this area there were few natural landing zones. It was both desirable and necessary to construct new landing zones with USAF-delivered weapons at places selected by the ground (RVNAF) and air (U.S. Army) mission commanders. Most of the landing zones used in Lam Son 719 were one-ship or two-ship LZs requiring hovering approaches and departures.[180]

Weather had a major effect on the timing of airmobile (helicopter) operations in support of Lam Son 719. Early morning fog, rain and cloud cover frequently delayed both airmobile and tactical air operations until late morning or early afternoon. Though the weather was rarely so bad as to preclude such operations for an entire day, occasionally airmobile operations were conducted under ceilings and weather conditions that prevented employment of close tactical air support.

In addition to the terrain and weather influences, the NVA air defenses in the area presented locally severe hazards to air operations. The NVA deployed throughout the operational area an extensive, well-integrated, highly mobile air defense system. Whenever possible, the enemy units employed their entire family of antiaircraft guns, field and infantry weapons against aircraft in the air and on the ground. The favored technique was to mass the antiaircraft weapons around friendly troop positions and areas that were to be used as helicopter landing and pick-up zones.[181/]

The ground fire environment threatening helicopters consisted primarily of 7.62mm small arms and automatic weapons such as 12.7mm machine guns. Although AAA (23mm or larger) was prevalent throughout the area, these more sophisticated weapons were seldom used against helicopters. They accounted for only four hits and three losses (the AAA threat is discussed in detail separately). In contrast, small arms (SA) and automatic weapons (AW) were responsible for 618 of the 695 hits reported. The majority of the losses were also due to SA and AW--44 losses to SA and 46 to AW. Once on the landing zone (LZ), the helicopters were subjected to a varied assortment of explosives, ranging from grenades to artillery. Mortars were responsible for the highest number of hits from this category.[182/]

As the campaign developed, the North Vietnamese relied heavily on mobility to counter helicopters. When they detected the location of a helicopter landing area, usually through Commando Vault drops and LZ preparations, the enemy would encircle the area. They stayed out of range while the area was prepared by tactical fighter strikes. After the LZ preparations, they rushed into the area with their small arms and automatic weapons setting up antiaircraft firing positions in anticipation of the coming helicopters. They normally held their fire while the helicopter reconnaissance teams tested the area and waited for the arrival of the lift aircraft. Then with coordinated barrage firing the enemy would try to drive the lift flights away completely, destroying as many as possible in the process. If this failed, or if they were not able to set up their AA positions quickly enough because the lift helicopters arrived at the LZ closely following the preparations, the enemy gunners used artillery and mortar fire to strike the helicopters as they were hovering to unload. The enemy troops moved in as close as possible to the friendly positions to achieve the greatest accuracy. This tactic of "hugging" friendly perimeters was especially effective where LZs served established South Vietnamese positions since it lessened the enemy's risk of tactical fighter strikes hitting him during the preparations for resupply or extraction lifts. Thus, every helicopter operation in the battle area had to be planned and conducted as a combat assault.[183/]

LANDING ZONE PREPARATIONS

The hazardous environment of the Lam Son 719 battle area and the large size of the airmobile operations required extensive and continuous coordination in the planning and execution of these operations. Integrating the efforts of the numerous combat and combat support elements to insure the success of the missions presented complex problems.

Prior to combat assaults, large resupply missions and heavy lift operations, air cavalry elements (helicopter reconnaissance and gunship teams) reconnoitered the flight routes to and from the objective area, tentatively selecting landing and pick-up zones, locating enemy forces and weapons positions and directing attacks by supporting firepower on the enemy targets. The air cavalry commander directed the preparatory and suppressive fires on the landing and pick-up zones, the approach and departure routes, and enemy positions in the objective area. The air cavalry commander normally was accompanied by an air artillery liaison officer and worked directly with a USAF forward air controller (FAC) flying overhead.[184/]

The destructive and suppressive firepower directed on the objective area by the air cavalry-forward air controller team included ground artillery, aerial rocket artillery, helicopter gunships, B-52 heavy bombers and tactical fighters. Though all available sources of firepower were utilized, the mass of destructive firepower was delivered by the USAF.

Seventh Air Force officials expressed concern to MACV and XXIV Corps planners in January over the serious AAA and small arms weapons threat existing in the Lam Son 719 AO. A plan for employing Arc Light sorties,

Commando Vault drops and tactical fighter strikes in a three-hour-long, carefully coordinated ordnance delivery for landing zone construction and preparation was presented to the Army planners.[185/] However, the Commanding Generals of I Corps and XXIV Corps did not accept this plan in its entirety until they had staggering losses at LZ Lo Lo.[186/] The Army officers placed first priority on completing combat assaults early in the day so that night defensive positions could be prepared during the daylight hours. They believed that the time required to implement the Air Force LZ preparation plan seriously delayed the combat assaults.

For the initial combat assaults into five different landing zones, on 8 February, the Army used 27 Arc Light sorties in the areas of potential landing zones, but only 12 tactical air strikes (10 on the Range LZ alone). Small arms and automatic weapons fire hit helicopters on three of the LZs. On 10 February, no Arc Light sorties hit in the vicinity of landing zone sites, but 10 tactical air strikes were used to suppress automatic weapons fire at LZ A Loui and 21 fighter sorties on LZ Delta. Most of these sorties were called in after the lift helicopters received small arms and automatic weapons fire. LZ Don was constructed with "Daisy Cutters" (MK 82, MK 83, and MK 84 bombs with fuze extenders) delivered by tactical fighter strikes over a five-hour period prior to the lift on 11 February. Often Commando Vault construction ordnance were dropped on the LZ sites many days before they were used. Throughout February the Army relied heavily on its artillery, ARA and gunships for LZ preparations using tactical air strikes primarily against known enemy locations. After 20 days of airmobile operations in Laos, 31 helicopters of all types had been lost by the allies and more than 230 had been damaged in combat.[187/]

Seventh Air Force reiterated their plan for preparing landing zones. It called for at least 15 Arc Light sorties delivering their bombs in an orderly pattern covering the objective area. The last Arc Light sortie was to complete its drop by 0700H. At first light, the Army Air Mission Commander and the USAF FAC would select the LZ site, mark it and bring in a fighter strike to "calibrate" the landing zone for the Commando Vault drop at about 0730H. Following the Commando Vault six or seven flights of fighters would refine the LZ construction with "daisy cutters" and suppress the LZ area with CBU ordnance. Finally, at least 15 sets of fighters were to deliver MK 82 (500 pound general purpose bomb) and BLU-27 (napalm) ordnance over a two-hour period to complete the suppression of enemy weapons. Just before the arrival of the lift helicopters, two fighters would drop CBU-12 (smoke) to screen the assault.[188/] The Army commanders did not seek the implementation of this LZ preparation plan in making the first of the "leap frog" combat assaults that would carry the battalions of the 1st Infantry Division to Tchepone. This assault was made at LZ Lo Lo on 3 March and proved to be so difficult and costly that its preparation demands a detailed description.

LZ Lo Lo

The FAC assigned to control the LZ preparation was Hammer 25 who reported on station at 0715H. Enroute to station, the FAC contacted the ABCCC Hillsboro and told the controller that mission numbers 5900, 5902, 5700, 5702, 6200, 5904, and 6644 were fragged to H-25. Hillsboro acknowledged the message. The FAC arrived on station and conducted a visual reconnaissance of the LZ area. At approximately 0800H, the FAC contacted Red Dragon 09 (U.S. Army Air Mission Commander) who informed the FAC where to put the ordnance around the LZ. Both the FAC and Red Dragon 09 informed Hillsboro of the urgent need for ordnance on the LZ. The FAC received and worked three missions on LZ construction and preparation employing part of the ordnance on the construction of the alternate LZ. These three missions consisted of four F-4 and two A-4 aircraft which delivered heavy ordnance (MK 82, MK 83, and MK 84, all with fuse extenders) in the LZ construction phase from 0806 to 0915H. The FAC did not observe any ground fire during these strikes. The primary LZ appeared adequate for 3-4 helicopters. Three A-7s were then employed in LZ preparation strikes delivering MK 82, MK 83 and CBU-24 munitions with strafing by 20mm guns. The CBU was used mainly to cover the helicopter approach area east of the LZ. The "hard bombs" were expended in tree lines north and south of the LZ. This was at the request of Red Dragon 09. A 0945H friendly artillery started coming in. With the A-7 sorties, LZ construction and preparation were completed and the FAC contacted Hillsboro and told them to send incoming "snake" (High Drag MK 82) and "nape" (BLU-27) to cover the helicopter assault. Hillsboro said a flight would check in shortly, just prior to helo assault. The FAC was replaced by Hammer 40. 189/

At approximately 1000H the assault began and helicopters reported taking fire from 200 meters northeast of the landing zone. As the assault progressed the helicopters reported incoming rockets and mortars from the south and southwest. Hammer 40 worked "snake and nape" on these positions at 1030H. The FAC informed Hillsboro that continuous tactical air would be needed to cover the assault. The FAC could not pinpoint any guns due to the foliage, though the helicopters were still taking fire after the 1030H strike. At 1050H Red Dragon 09 requested more tactical air strikes in the tree line southeast and southwest of the LZ about 800 meters. The FAC had radio problems and could only transmit on UHF with Hammer Control and the fighters. The FAC could monitor conversation between Hammer Control and the helicopters on FM and between Hammer Control and Hillsboro on VHF. The ground commander requested close-in support; and the FAC, after conferring with Red Dragon 09 on smoke and obtaining the ground commander's initials for close support clearance, directed an F-4 flight to strike in the trees 100 meters south of the friendlies. The strike of two F-4s went in at 1130H. All bombs were on target and resulted in a large white secondary explosion. The ground commander relayed through Red Dragon 09 that tactical air should be used south along the tree line again. The FAC worked two more sets of fighters till 1200H when he briefed Hammer 21 on the situation and returned to his base. The weather was clear with five miles visibility.

The combat assault was interrupted by enemy fire after 19 helicopters had delivered their troop loads. A total of 20 fighters expended "snake and nape" and strafed the area southeast and southwest of the LZ between 1030H and 1324H when the assault was again attempted. Hammer 21 rendezvoused with Hammer 40 at 1150H and was briefed on the heavy automatic weapons fire from south and southeast of the LZ. Between 1210H and 1324H the FAC directed 10 F-4s and two A-4 strikes with "snake and nape" on these positions. The friendly troops were unable to mark this position because of the close proximity of the enemy. The FAC was finding the friendly positions by low passes and marking for the fighters by rocking his wings. The helicopters approaching LZ Lo Lo continued to receive heavy ground fire, despite efforts by the FAC, fighters and helicopter gunships. The FAC was then replaced by Hammer 222.

Hammer 222 placed 10 fighter strikes with "snake and nape" south of the primary LZ between 1350H and 1455H. He was relieved by Hammer 48. Until 1555H when Hammer 48 spotted an enemy mortar position on the face of the escarpment north of LZ Lo Lo, the FACs had not seen any enemy positions but had directed their strikes on targets described by helicopter crews and the ground commander.

Hammer 48 reported the active mortar position to Red Dragon 09, but he was told not to direct tactical fighters on the enemy position. So the FAC left the area and went to the vicinity of FSB Delta to work with the 190/ Marines.

The helicopter lifts into LZ Lo Lo began again at 1600H and the assault was completed at 1830H.

Summary

The site of LZ Lo Lo was selected by the U.S. Army Air Mission Commander at 0800H. The FAC was informed of the selection and requested to put in ordnance. Beginning at 0806H six fighters delivered 14 MK 82 (500 pound, general purpose), seven MK 83 (1000 pound, general purpose) and eight MK 84 (2000 pound, general purpose) bombs all with fuse extenders to clear the LZ area of obstructions. Then at 0930H three fighters delivered antipersonnel munitions (eight MK 82, two MK 83, 16 CBU-24) and strafed with 20mm guns as final preparation for the combat assault into the LZ. No enemy fire was observed. The assault began at 1000H and immediately the lift helicopters were hit by automatic weapons and mortars. Four of the first 19 helicopters to be inserted were shot down on the LZ, and others received hits causing heavy battle damage.

The assault was stopped and for the next six hours, 30 more tactical air sorties struck the LZ area along with helicopter gunships and artillery.

The lift was completed at 1830H. Forty-two helicopters had been hit, 20 shot down and 7 destroyed in the operation. During the night of 2-3 March, eight Arc Light sorties had been placed on points south of the LZ. The closest strike was put one kilometer south of Lo Lo at 0455H. Figure 15 illustrates the Arc Light target pattern for each of the Landing Zones discussed.

LZ Liz

After the costly and frustrating combat assault into LZ Lo Lo, the proposed LZ prep plan developed by 7AF was accepted by XXIV Corps, and deliberate preparation and greater caution were employed in the lift on 4 March into LZ Liz. The LZ site had been cleared by a Commando Vault (BLU-82) drop on 1 March. Fourteen Arc Light sorties hit the area dropping in a rectangular pattern about the primary and alternate LZs. The last sortie delivered its bombs at 0635H. The FACs began directing four fighter strikes with heavy LZ construction ordnance on an alternate LZ at 0717H on 4 March. Between 0815H and 0845H they put in six fighters with heavy ordnance on the primary LZ and at 0915H began the final preparation with antipersonnel munitions. Thirteen sorties were used in this phase completing the preparation at 0945H. All was in readiness by 1000H in the judgment of the FAC, but the U.S. Army Air Mission Commander had not yet arrived. A continuous arc of fire burned from the north around the west to the south side of the LZ. The fire burned intensely and set up a smoke screen. The wind blew from the east. The weather in the area was hazy with 3 to 4 miles visibility. However, the lift helicopters were being held at Khe Sanh by low ceilings and poor visibility.[191/]

While waiting for the arrival of the helicopters, the FACs continued to place tactical air strikes about the LZ approximately every 10 minutes from 1000H to 1500H. The smoke and haze reduced the visibility to one quarter of a mile.

The helicopter assault was delayed from 1330H to 1430H by the Air Mission Commander because the FAC did not consider the LZ clear at this time. Then at 1430H it was again delayed because the reconnaissance

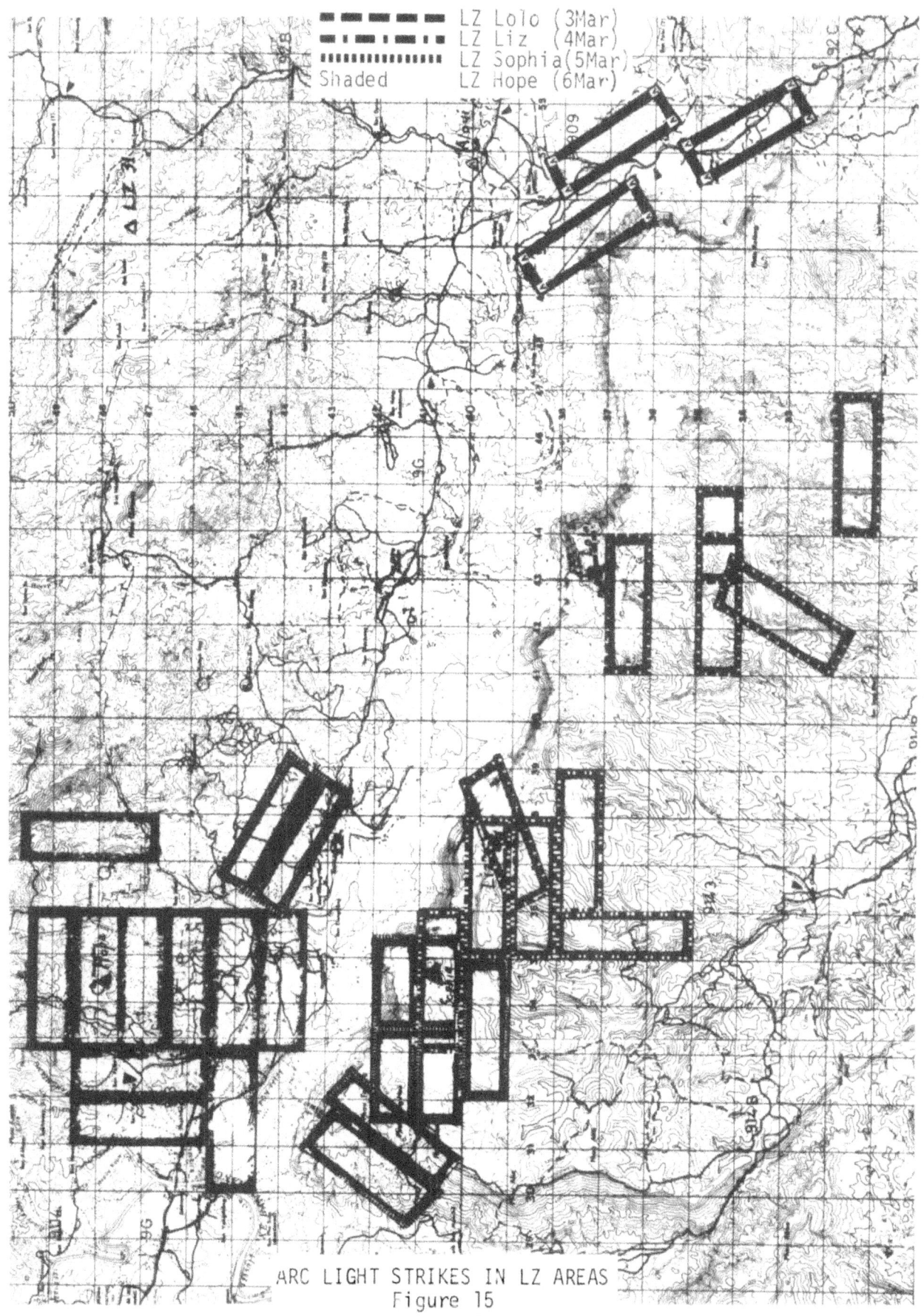

ARC LIGHT STRIKES IN LZ AREAS
Figure 15

helicopters drew machine gun fire 600 meters south and east of the LZ. The reconnaissance and tactical air strikes continued until the combat assault began at 1715H. A total of 61 fighter sorties were used over 10 hours to prepare the landing zone. An additional nine sorties dropped suppressive munitions during the assault which was completed at 1815H.[192/]

Despite this extensive preparation enemy automatic weapons took their toll. Sixty-five troop lift helicopters participated in the assault of which 18 were hit. Two of these were destroyed.[193/]

LZ Sophia

On 5 March a combat assault of two infantry battalions was made at LZ Sophia. Sixteen Arc Light sorties struck the western end of the escarpment in an orderly pattern during the night and early morning with the last sortie striking at 0740H. Beginning at 0814H the FAC directed three fighters with LZ construction ordnance on the LZ site. The combat assault was scheduled for 0900H but at 0830H it was put on a weather hold because of low ceilings and poor visibility at the pick-up zone and landing zone. Low clouds over the landing zone site were also preventing the FAC from delivering the preparation ordnance on schedule. However, the assault did not begin until 1325H allowing a total of 35 tactical air strikes to hit the LZ area in preparation for the helicopters. During this six hours the cloud coverage varied from 1/8 to 6/8 with the bases at 7,000 feet and the tops at 9,000 feet MSL and the visibility was four miles with smoke and haze.[194/]

The first helicopter arrived at the LZ at 1325H. Two F-4s delivered

CBU-12 (antipersonnel and smoke ordnance) at 1330H on the edge of the landing zone.[195/] The assault continued until 1740H with six fighter sorties striking the area during the lift operation.

Three lift helicopters were downed by enemy fire.[196/]

LZ Hope

The final combat assault in the series of "leap frogging" maneuvers occurred in the Tchepone area at LZ Hope on 6 March. It also was a two-battalion lift.

Twenty-five Arc Light sorties struck the Tchepone area about the primary and secondary landing zone sites during the night of 5-6 March with the last of these preparatory strikes hitting at 0620H.

The initial tactical air strikes were directed on the selected primary LZ site at 0720H. From 0720H to 0816H seven fighters delivered heavy LZ construction ordnance on the site. At 0817H a Commando Vault drop hit 300 meters north of the site being constructed by the FAC. The Commando Vault cleared an area on ground with a greater slope than the site already under construction. The FAC continued to work the originally selected site with 6 more fighters delivering construction ordnance on it to blow away the dense foliage. At 0912H a Commando Vault was dropped to clear an alternate LZ (Victory). The bomb hit 400 meters north of the planned coordinates but cleared a good site suitable for 3-4 helicopters. From 0925H to 0957H, eight fighters dropped antipersonnel munitions on the primary LZ. Thus a total of 21 tactical air strikes were used in the LZ construction plus two Commando Vault drops. Suppressive ordnance (primarily hard bombs and napalm) was dropped by 24 more fighter sorties. The preparation of the landing zone ended at 1215H, with the drop of CBU-12 (smoke) by four F-4 aircraft. The combat assault began immediately following the smoke drop. Twenty-nine tactical air strikes hit the area during the troop lift which ended at 1343H.[197/]

The lift helicopters departed from a pick-up zone in the Khe Sanh area and flew in a corridor over Landing Zones Hotel, Delta I, Brown, Lo Lo, Liz and Sophia. The helicopters began to let down at Liz enroute to Sophia turning north of Sophia to the Hope LZ. Two battalions of infantry were delivered in two waves of over 60 helicopters each. The only helicopter loss resulted from a hit over Sophia. It was downed but later managed to fly back to Khe Sanh.[198/]

RESUPPLY AND EXTRACTION

There were no more major combat assaults after the one at LZ Hope. Yet the resupply, medical evacuation and troop extraction missions proved to be just as hazardous if less dramatic.

The heavy equipment, conex containers and artillery pieces to construct the fire support bases were brought in by helicopters. The fuel, food, water, ammunition and bulk supplies necessary to sustain the South Vietnamese troops were also brought in by helicopters. Virtually all of the infantry entered Laos by helicopter and more than three-quarters of them left aboard helicopters. Over 22,000 helicopter sorties were flown moving personnel and supplies in Laos. The USAF provided firepower support for these operations when called upon to do so by the Army. The enemy frequently made it very difficult to get helicopters into landing zones with his encirclement and "hugging" tactics.

The medical evacuation of 122 wounded rangers on 22 February could not be effected until three Arc Light sorties and 46 tactical air strikes hit the pick up zone. Subsequently the 21st Ranger Battalion was forced to abandon its position because enemy fire had prevented helicopter resupply for several days. On 4 March, the commander of an airborne battalion located five kilometers north of FSB A Loui requested that the FAC flying over his position pass the following message to the Commanding General of the Airborne Division:[199/]

> *"Under siege for 10 days, negative resupply, 200 killed and wounded. 10 APC and 3 tanks of friendlies destroyed. No food and water for last two days. Urgently request medevac helicopters, resupply and Hammer FAC and fast movers at first light. During siege friendlies and gunships have destroyed 14 enemy tanks and killed hundreds of NVA."*

He waited another day before any relief arrived. As the campaign progressed, the inability to effect helicopter resupply made this a recurring story and rendered some positions untenable. FSB Lo Lo's abandonment on 15 March was due in part to the enemy's disruption of resupply and medical evacuation efforts despite 15 Arc Light and 55 tactical air strikes on enemy positions. On 22 March after 22 Arc Light and 40 tactical air sorties, neither resupply nor extraction by helicopter could be accomplished at FSB Delta and the Marines evacuated the position.

CLOSE AIR SUPPORT

Except for the specific missions to construct landing zones, it was difficult to distinguish between fire suppression strikes about the LZs and close air support of the RVNAF troops. Less than three percent of the total tactical air sortie efforts went into landing zone construction as such but 42 percent of the effort went against enemy personnel and nearly nine percent against enemy storage areas and fortifications.[200/] The fact that the outnumbered South Vietnamese forces relied heavily on air delivered fire power to preserve their position, kill enemy troops and destroy enemy installations has been described in Chapter III. Figure A-2 shows the sorties flown in Lam Son 719 against personnel. The total daily number includes the sorties flown against confirmed and suspected enemy locations as well as those which supported troops in contact (TIC). The sorties against personnel varied with the level of enemy activity. As the enemy pressure mounted, the number of sorties against personnel rose from a low of 10 on 9 February to a high of 185 on 17 March. TICs had the highest priority among the targets for tactical air and of the 3593 anti-personnel sorties, 588 fighter and 90 gunship missions flew in direct support of troops in contact.[201/] Most enemy attacks were broken only by the repeated, accurate delivery of tactical air strikes on the enemy troops. The FAC's role in marking the targets, requesting proper ordnance and coordinating with the friendly ground commanders was absolutely critical in the close air support operations. Despite the language difficulties, the FACs proved capable of filling the void created by the lack of tactical air control parties on the ground in the battle area.

During the period when the area of operations was at its largest, six FACs worked in sectors during the day with an additional FAC flying as an artillery spotter. At this time Seventh Air Force allocated a flight of fighters every ten minutes to the Lam Son 719 operation. FACs who were supporting ground units under attack occasionally had as many as six flights of fighters on station over the AO.[202/] To effectively employ the weapons system required a thorough knowledge by the FAC of the various fighters and the delivery modes for their ordnance. When the enemy launched his final major offensive to destroy the South Vietnamese force and engaged all of the friendly units, problems of congested airspace, overloaded communication channels and priority of strikes developed. Yet the skill and dedication of the FACs and the fighter crews prevented any midair collisions and delivered the air strikes so well that the enemy failed in his objectives.

At night three FACs were always on station with gunships (AC-130 or AC-119) and flareships (C-123) available to each of them. Most of the sorties in the Lam Son 719 AO were in support of TICs, but they also struck tanks and other vehicles.

Time after time in Lam Son 719 tactical air support was vital to the ground combat situation. The battle at Objective 31 on 25 February discussed in Chapter III is just one example of the critical role played by tactical air strikes in close support operations. It was described by the Director of DASC Victor as follows:[203]

> ...Tac air was used against enemy troops coming up into the wire attacking in the daytime primarily from the northeast of LZ 31 on the first day. When they were far enough away from the friendly troops, by 800 meters or so, CBU-24 was employed on them as well as some 2000-pound bombs or daisy cutters with extended fuses until the ground commander asked that they not be used any more. They were a safe distance away but the blast and noise was disconcerting to the friendly troops...Tac air kept pounding all day long the entire period. When darkness came and the fighters could not be practically employed in a night owl operation in close proximity, gunships were brought on station and they fired constantly throughout the night. They expended seven gunships and sufficient flareships to flare on the gunships the first night. We had sufficient and ample gunships readily available on station to take over when one gunship expended its ordnance or a flareship ran out of flares. This became critical. In between gunships, three to four minutes, the enemy would be up and into the wire. The gunship would then shoot them back from the wire and do this until the next gunship came up. It continued all night. There is no doubt in my mind that Hill 31 would have been overrun that first day or at least that first night, if it had not been for tac air and gunships...

The Hammer FAC Daily Intelligence Summaries are filled with examples of FACs bringing in fighters very close to friendly troops. On 4 March, Hammer 223 was flying north of A Loui when his Vietnamese back seater received word from the ground commander that he was in a heavy TIC situation. The FAC expended three sets of fighters with what the ground commander called good accuracy. Shortly after, the ground commander, a

Major Phu, said the TIC was broken. His troops moved into the bombed area and found 150 dead NVA soldiers, along with small arms, machine guns and rockets. Three dazed and wounded prisoners were captured.[204/] In a less spectacular, but perhaps more typical strike on 28 February, Hammer 224 had a call at 0730 from a ground commander reporting contact with the enemy about six kilometers south of Route 9 near the border. An NVA company was in bunkers with small arms, automatic weapons and mortars. The friendlies were to the north and had their position marked with a red panel. The FAC requested napalm and Snakeye 500-pound bombs from Hillsboro, the ABCCC, and put in three sets of fighters with "snake and nape." The friendlies further marked their positions with smoke, and as the ground commander adjusted the fire through the back seater, the bombs were put right on target. A large and a small secondary explosion were reported, and the bombs also uncovered 20 bunkers and trenches under trees. An hour later, the ground commander was attacked again and the FAC was overhead with a set of fighters, putting them very close to the friendly positions marked with violet smoke. One napalm cannister burst very close to friendlies, but there were no casualties. Ground forces counted 12 KBA after the strike.[205/]

In the hectic last days of withdrawal, tac air and B-52s worked together to preserve an ARVN battalion position until helicopters could get the surviving members to safety. Hammer 223 on the early morning of the 20th of March, was over the battalion south of FSB A Loui, when he was informed of a TIC situation. An Arc Light was put in just 300 meters from the friendly battalion. In five minutes, after the smoke and dust of the B-52 strike had cleared, the FAC immediately started putting in fighters, nine sets of them, resulting in numerous secondary explosions and fires just outside the friendly perimeter. The battalion commander had insisted on these strikes very close to his position and the FAC double-checked with Hammer Control to make sure it was safe. When the strikes were over and the fighters had left, the ground commander reported that "the enemy was still taking fire," meaning that secondary explosions kept going off. The FAC destroyed a sizable ammunition storage area with these strikes.[206/]

Most of the close air support sorties were flown by F-100 and F-4 aircraft delivering "snake and nape" ordnance in a low angle mode. The gunships employed their standard configurations of 7.62mm, 20mm or 40mm weapons. The aircrews and FACs reported 2406 personnel killed by tactical air strikes.[207/] In addition to those killed there was an unknown number of enemy soldiers wounded and a significant quantity of weapons, ammunition and combat equipment destroyed.

In concluding this discussion of close air support, it must be noted that just as intensive tactical air strikes could not wholly suppress enemy weapons fire on helicopters neither could it prevent a friendly ground position from being overrun. Careful examination of the battles at Ranger Hill, Objective 31, FSB Lo Lo and FSB Delta show that when the enemy had numerical superiority and was determined to take a position, tactical air power alone could not stop him from doing so once the ground defense was weakened.

The efficient employment of tactical air resources in the close support operations was affected by a variety of factors. The dense vegetation, low clouds and poor low altitude visibility presented technical problems for the aircrews and FACs. The allocation of strike aircraft and ordnance among competing requests posed problems of command and control. The F-100 and F-4 aircraft had limitations in on-station loiter time and ordnance carrying capacity which made it necessary to generate a high number of sorties in order to meet the ground forces' requirements of responsiveness in time and ordnance. A weapons platform with considerably longer loiter time and a greater capacity for carrying a variety of ordnance and equal survivability would have been very useful in meeting the firepower needs of the ground forces in the changing battle situation.

ATTACKS AGAINST AIR DEFENSES

More than 15 percent of the tactical air sorties in Lam Son 719 went against enemy antiaircraft weapons. As Seventh Air Force officials knew very well, the NVA had a formidable air defense network deployed along the logistics route structure in southern Laos. When warned of the threat, allied Army commanders failed to share the Air Force's concern.[208/] While adhering to the Army's priorities in tactical air support, the Air Force conducted a concerted "gun killing" effort throughout the campaign. As a result of these operations 109 antiaircraft artillery pieces were destroyed, 18 damaged and 42 silenced. Additionally, 54 automatic weapons were destroyed, 9 damaged and 10 silenced. Mortar and artillery positions threatening helicopter landing zones were also struck. A total of 225 weapons were destroyed, 48 damaged and 63 silenced by tactical air.[209]

Defenses Against Fixed Wing Aircraft

The principal threat to fixed wing aircraft from antiaircraft guns consisted of 57mm, 37mm, and 23mm. The predominant caliber encountered was the 37mm gun. At the onset of the operation, there were an estimated 155 antiaircraft guns in the Lam Son 719 area, 60 percent of which were 37mm. Near the end of the operation the estimated gun count had decreased by 20 guns to 135, indicating that the enemy's losses of antiaircraft weapons from air strikes had exceeded his capability to replace them.

It was not possible to estimate the number of automatic weapons (12.7mm and 14.5mm) in the area of operations because of their mobility; however, these guns posed the most significant threat. Automatic weapons were known to be associated with AAA units and infantry units as well, and were deployed throughout the Lam Son 719 AO. These weapons were credited with the largest number of hits and losses.

There were a total of 42 fixed-wing hits and seven fixed wing aircraft losses. These figures reflect 3.4 hits per 1000 sorties and .58 losses per 1000 sorties, and compare with 1.0 hits per 1000 sorties and .24 losses per 1000 sorties in Steel Tiger during November, December, and January.[210]

While electronic and photographic reconnaissance yielded some indications that there were fire control radars in the Lam Son 719 area, none was confirmed. There were no reported radar-directed AAA firings in the Lam Son 719 AO.

Defense Against Helicopters

The helicopters most vulnerable to enemy ground fire were those engaged in inserting or extracting troops. The largest number of hits were taken by the UH-1Hs, which carried the troops, and the AH-1Gs which flew gunship escorts. During the period 8 February to 24 March, 631 helicopters sustained hits by enemy ground-to-air fire. This resulted in U.S. forces losing 103 helicopters in combat operations. The overall statistics reveal a hit rate of 10.3 per 1000 sorties in the Lam Son 719 AO in Laos and a loss rate of 1.8 per 1000 sorties.*

Weapons Employed Against Defenses

There were 1284 sorties against enemy air defenses; of these, 738 sorties struck automatic weapons and small arms positions. Most of the sorties were to suppress enemy gunfire rather than to "kill" the gun. The

---

*As noted earlier, a helicopter frequently logged several sorties on one mission. For example, on a typical mission a helicopter departed Quang Tri, refueled at Vandegrift FSB, refueled at Khe Sanh, flew to a troop pick up point, carried the troops to an LZ, and then returned to Quang Tri again by way of Khe Sanh and Vandegrift. On such a mission, the helicopter would log seven sorties. Thus, Army helicopter sortie rates can in no way be compared with Air Force sortie rates.

primary munitions used in the suppression strikes were CBU-24, CBU-49, and BLU 27. These munitions could kill and wound the gunners, but not destroy the weapons.

Direct hits in the gun pit by hard bombs were required to destroy antiaircraft artillery pieces (such as 23mm, 37mm or 57mm). It was very difficult to hit a camouflaged gun surrounded by dense vegetation which was the typical emplacement in Lam Son 719, because it presented a very small target.

The most efficient weapon used against these small, obscure targets was the Paveway, a laser-guided MK 84 or M118 bomb. The illuminator aircraft flew at 8000 feet as the strike aircraft released the ordnance in a 45-degree dive at 450 knots from 12,000 feet altitude. Using this delivery mode, both aircraft were beyond the lethal range of all but the largest of the enemy's AA pieces. During the 8 February - 24 March period, 99 sorties attacked antiaircraft artillery sites delivering 173 laser-guided bombs resulting in 70 AA positions destroyed and five damaged.[211/]

One USAF Hammer FAC who had developed a special skill in knocking out AA weapons was First Lieutenant Leonard J. Funderburk. Prior to Lam Son 719, he was credited with 75 guns destroyed in Laos and during the operation, he added another 47. His method was to request Paveway ordnance as soon as he arrived on station and began his visual reconnaissance. By the time the fighters arrived, he would have pinpointed the targets usually by observing the location of muzzle flashes. He would direct the strike on the gun position and immediately request another set of fighters equipped with Paveway ordnance. He considered Paveway not only the best weapon against AA weapons but also the best against moving or stationary tanks.[212/]

ATTACKS AGAINST ARMOR

Perhaps the most dramatic episodes for tactical air power during Lam Son 719 occurred in the attacks on enemy tanks. One of the surprising developments in the operation was the deployment of a tank regiment in the battle area. It is estimated that there were 120 tanks including the PT-76, T-34 and T-54 models.[213/]

The PT-76 is a light, amphibious tank weighing 15.4 tons and armed with a 76mm main gun plus one 7.62mm machine gun mounted coaxially with the main gun. The T-34 is a medium tank weighing 35 tons when combat loaded and armed with a 85mm main gun. The T-54 is a medium class tank weighing 40 tons and armed with one 100mm main gun, one 12.7mm (.50 caliber) machine gun mounted on the turret roof and two 7.62mm machine guns, one mounted coaxially with the main gun and one mounted in the front of the hull. Most of the tanks in the Lam Son 719 area were PT-76s; however, the T-54 presented the greatest challenge to tactical air, not only because of its heavier armor, but its 12.7mm machine gun with a 1000-meter effective range gave the tank crews the capability to shoot down aircraft that made low-altitude passes on them.[214]

The tanks were intended to provide mobile firepower support of the NVA infantry as compensation for the U.S. air-delivered firepower supporting the ARVN. The destruction of these tanks was of importance throughout the campaign but critically so during the battle for Objective 31 and in the final days of the retreat.

Throughout the whole of the campaign the allies claimed the destruction of 108 enemy tanks. Tactical air strikes destroyed 74 and damaged 24 others in 241 attacks made during the critical period of fighting, 8 February to 24 March. (See Figure 16.) These attacks, in effect, neutralized the NVA tank regiment, denying the enemy what he undoubtedly considered a critical advantage against the South Vietnamese forces. Tactical air also was used on 24 March to knock out the usable tanks left behind by the withdrawing ARVN forces.

Since it was impossible to predict the time and location of enemy tank appearances, they were attacked by whatever strike aircraft and ordnance were available when they were sighted. Consequently, the greatest number of attacks were made with 500 pound general purpose bombs (MK 82) and napalm (BLU-27), either singly or in combination, because more than half of the daily fighter sorties carried this ordnance. There were 134 attacks made with these bombs resulting in 28 tanks destroyed and nine damaged.

Rockeye II (MK 20; antiarmor, cluster bomblet) and CBU-24 munitions used in combination with general purpose bombs were delivered in 49 attacks and destroyed 11 tanks, while damaging seven others. In four attacks CBU-24s alone were dropped and one tank was destroyed. The Zuni rocket (5 inch, folding fin, aerial rocket with 15 pound shaped charge) demonstrated its effectiveness in destroying four tanks in four attacks.

The Paveway again proved to be a very efficient weapon. Despite the protection of camouflage, terrain cover and movement, seven enemy tanks were destroyed by the laser-guided bombs. In six attacks delivering 10 MK 84 LGBs five tanks were destroyed (the one tank was missed because of a "bore-sight" error in the illuminator). Two attacks with two M118 LGB weapons destroyed two tanks. A Hammer FAC described the efficiency of the Paveway:[215/]

> ...I put in two sets of conventional ordnance on this one tank, a set of A-37s and a set of F-100s with negative results. They got all around it, but didn't even knock the camouflage off the tank. I received a flight of Paveways, and with the first bomb, it was destroyed. The tank rolled over on its side and it was seen burning...

In addition to its high-kill ratio, the Paveway was less dangerous to deliver against a T-54 with its turret mounted machine gun. The delivery mode was the same as that employed against the antiaircraft guns; that is, the laser-guided bombs were released by the strike aircraft in a 45 degree dive at 450 knots calibrated airspeed and 12000 feet

ATTACKS AGAINST ENEMY TANKS

(8 FEB-24 MAR 71)

ORDNANCE	ATTACKS	DESTROYED	DAMAGED	SF/E*	RNO**
MK-82 HD/BLU-27	47	10	4	39	6
20MM HEI/API & 7.6MM (AC-119K)	11	10	1	18	
MK-82/CBU-24	24	4	4	11	3
MK-82/MK-20 (ROCKEYE)	22	5	2	1	4
MK-84 LGB	6	5			
MK-82/LAU-10 (ZUNI)	4	4			
MK-82/(NAPALM)	24	7	4	2	2
MK-83/CBU-24	3	2	1		
MK-82	44	3		1	11
BLU-27	6	2			
40MM HEI (AC-130)	28	14	3	3	
CBU-24	4	1		1	
AGM-62-A	3				3
NAPALM	1	1			
M-118 LGB	2	2			
MK-82/MK-81	7	4	3	8	
MK-82 HD	2		1		
MK-82/20MM	3		1	6	
TOTALS	241	74	24	90	29

* Secondary fires and explosions

** Results not observed

Figure 16

altitude with the illuminator aircraft at 8000 feet. On the other hand, hard bombs and napalm had to be delivered in a low angle, low altitude mode which placed the fighter in the fire envelope of the 12.7mm machine gun.

Tanks encountered at night were engaged by the AC-119K and AC-130 gunships. In 11 attacks, AC-119K aircrews reported destroying 10 tanks and damaging one with 20mm HEI/API (high explosive incendiary/armor piercing incendiary) munitions. AC-130 crews firing 40mm HEI destroyed 14 tanks and damaged three others in 28 attacks. All of these tanks are believed to have been PT-76 light tanks. The AC-130 results were reported by either FACs or ground reconnaissance. The AC-119K crews used the criteria that impacts on the target which resulted in secondary explosions or fires destroyed the target and impacts on the target with no target reaction are reported as damaged. The AC-130 firings were from 9500 feet AGL and the AC-119K attacks were from 5500 feet AGL. Both used normal gunship firing tactics.[216/]

Tactical air achieved a stunning success overall in the destruction of the enemy's armored force, yet in localized situations, low cloud cover and poor visibility did permit the enemy to maneuver his tanks unseen from the air. This gave him an advantage at Objective 31 and could have (save for a break-in-the-weather) on 22 March when he massed 20 tanks and sought to overtake the ARVN armored column.

INTERDICTION

To reduce the combat effectiveness of the North Vietnamese Army in the Lam Son 719 area, an extensive air effort was directed at denying logistical support to the troops on the battlefield, by striking trucks, supply and storage areas, and by interdicting the lines of communication supporting movement into the Lam Son 719 area.

Storage area targets within the AO were developed from visual and photo reconnaissance and other sources of information. These base camp, truck park and storage area destruction operations have already been described in Chapter III. However, it should be noted that more than six percent (538 sorties) of the tactical air strikes in the Lam Son 719 campaign were directed against these targets and accounted for much of the destroyed supplies and equipment listed in the BDA Table of the statistical appendix.

There were 1111 tactical air sorties which struck LOC interdiction targets. They represented 13 percent of the Lam Son 719 effort and resulted in 316 route cuts and road slides. Allied to this effort were the truck-killing operations. There were 1433 sorties flown against vehicles in the Lam Son 719 AO. The aircrews and FACs reported 1539 trucks destroyed and 485 damaged by these strikes.[217/]

The effects of the attacks against trucks and storage areas and route interdiction cannot be measured solely in quantitative terms.

Prisoners reported that NVA units were frequently short of food, ammunition, medical supplies and POL. Some NVA units were forced to avoid combat for a time because of casualties and inadequate logistical support. It is believed that the effects of air and ground attacks on the enemy limited the duration of sustained offensives. NVA offensive operations involved only two weeks of the six week campaign. 218/

ARC LIGHT

During Lam Son 719, B-52s were heavily committed in support of the campaign. The B-52 aircraft, located at U-Tapao Airfield, Thailand, flew 1358 sorties between 8 February and 24 March. The peak of the effort occurred between 4 and 8 March during the "leap frog" push to Tchepone and the searching operation in the Tchepone area.

The initial planning for the application of B-52s in support of Lam Son 719 was accomplished at Seventh Air Force headquarters. A study was prepared and then presented to Lieutenant General Sutherland at his XXIV Corps Forward Headquarters which proposed the employment of blocking strikes against the enemy LOCs into the planned battle area. This proposal was approved and implemented. After the ground offensive was launched on 8 February, the target selection for the Lam Son 719 B-52 sorties was done almost entirely by Lieutenant General Lam, Commanding General of the South Vietnamese forces in the operation. Seventh Air Force sent an Arc Light liaison officer to Quang Tri to brief the Allied Corps commanders and staffs on B-52 operating and targeting procedures.

Through the liaison established during this visit, Arc Light target boxes nominated from the Seventh Air Force intelligence data base and photo interpretation were forwarded to XXIV Corps. However, General Lam personally made the daily target selections for the B-52 sorties allocated to the Lam Son 719 operation by MACV.[219]

The usual method of selecting targets based upon hard intelligence was modified in favor of using B-52s in direct support of the ground troops. This led to some novel tactics by the ARVN in their use of heavy strategic bombers. Capitalizing on the NVA tactic of "hugging" the friendly positions (sometimes as close as 30 meters), the 1st Infantry Division would set up night defensive positions out from the fire support bases and request an Arc Light strike on their NDP coordinates during the early morning hours. About one-half hour before the scheduled time-over-target, the infantrymen would withdraw from their position hoping that the Arc Light strike would find the NVA troops still in the vicinity of the night position.[220] It frequently worked. Variations of this tactic were also employed during the day. At LZ Lo Lo, Brigadier General Phan Van Phu, Commander of the 1st Infantry Division reported, "The enemy tries to get very close to us, hoping we will get hit by one of our own bombs. We let them come close, then pull back just before the air strikes, closing again when the bombers have finished. If you want to kill people, you must use maximum air."[221]

In another statement, General Phu added, "During the heavy fighting around FSB Lo Lo early in the week, I called for B-52 strikes within 300 yards of my unit. Many of the nearly 1700 enemy soldiers reported killed in that fighting died in those strikes." [222/] Some of the more spectacular "kills" of enemy troops by Arc Light have already been described in Chapter III.

The B-52s were also targeted against storage areas, base camps, troop concentrations, interdiction points and anticipated landing zone areas. RVNAF units searched in only 40 of the 617 Arc Light target areas struck in Lam Son 719. [223/] The total ground confirmed Arc Light bomb damage as reported on 24 March included 2194 enemy killed by air and the destruction of 65 vehicles, 957 structures, 439 crew served weapons, 1711 individual weapons, 852 tons of ammunition and 1176 tons of rice.* [224/]

In order to provide the greatest possible responsiveness to the firepower needs of the ground commander, SAC developed special strike planning procedures which allowed target changes as late as three hours prior to the time-over-target. The Seventh Air Force B-52 defensive support aircraft were reprogrammed to meet the bombers' flexibility.

To increase the Arc Light striking force, the daily sortie rate was raised from 33 to 40 on 24 February. Later, the bombers were reconfigured to enable them to carry greater bomb loads. Initially each bomber carried

---

*As previously noted, tac air hit many of the same targets as the B-52s. Therefore, it frequently was not really possible to discriminate between B-52 and tac air bomb damage.

119

66 bombs consisting of 24 MK 82 (500 pound, general purpose) and 42 M117 (750 pounds, general purpose) bombs. On 6 March one cell (three B-52s) was configured to carry 108 bombs (84 MK 82s and 24 M117s) per aircraft. One additional bomber each day for the remainder of the operation was converted to carry 108 bombs. During the period 8 February to 24 March, B-52s delivered 9,219 tons of 500 pound bombs and 23,183 tons of 750 pound bombs for a total of 32,402 tons of ordnance dropped in support of Lam Son 719.

SHORT ROUNDS

There were three incidents in which the ordnance from tactical air strikes struck allied ground positions in Operation Lam Son 719. (30 January to 24 March). The first incident occurred on 6 February when a Navy A-6, Electron 512, dropped two Rockeye II (antiarmor CBU) dispensers on friendly positions near Lao Bao in Quang Tri Province, Republic of Vietnam. The ordnance hit elements of the 8th Airborne Battalion. Seven ARVN soldiers were killed, 55 were wounded and one armored personnel carrier was destroyed. The cause of the short round was attributed to poor weather requiring internal electrical guidance for expenditure of the Rockeye. Aircrew disorientation, target misidentification and possible equipment malfunction contributed to the incident.[225/]

Insertions into Landing Zone Lo Lo on 5 March resulted in 38 ARVN injured in another short round incident. Two F-4 aircraft, Gunfighter 26 and 27, from the 366th Tactical Fighter Wing expended CBU-12 white phosphorous incendiary smoke during the insertion.[226/]

On 14 March, two Marine A-4E aircraft, Ring Neck 203-1 and 203-2 from the 1st MAW dropped Mark 82, 500 pound high-drag bombs on a friendly position of the First ARVN Infantry Division resulting in nine killed, 13 wounded seriously and three with minor injuries. Poor communications between the FAC and the ground commander, uncertainty of the exact location of the friendly forces and weather conditions were primary factors contributing to the incident. Due to an uncooperative attitude by the FAC's Vietnamese interpreter, the FAC had to use an Army helicopter as relay in communicating with the ground commander. The exact friendly position was impossible to establish during the investigation. The friendly commander did acknowledge, however, that the FAC's smoke was on the enemy position. The FAC was IFR during the final run in of Ring Neck 203-2 and unable to observe the strike. During the last portion of his final, Ring Neck 203-2 was hit by enemy ground fire which could have affected his accuracy of release.227/

AIRCRAFT LOSSES

Seven U.S. tactical aircraft were lost to enemy fire during Lam Son 719. The pertinent data are depicted on the following table and map. Five of the losses were strike aircraft. This loss rate was considered low in view of the more than 8000 strike sorties flown and, perhaps more significant, the more than 24,000 passes made by fighters against targets that were well defended by antiaircraft weapons. (See Figures 17 and 18.)

IMPLICATIONS FOR FUTURE OPERATIONS

In Operation Lam Son 719 all of the complex facets of the Second Indochina War appear in kaleidoscopic patterns. But, of special interest to the U.S. Air Force, are the implications for future operations arising from the experiences of supporting a corps-size ground force of an allied nation given air mobility by the U.S. Army. These Air Force experiences need analysis and reflection beyond this contemporary report's limitations of time and scope. Nonetheless, certain implications seem apparent.

1. To conduct a corps-size operation there must be detailed planning at all levels of command. It is especially important that there be thorough planning for contingencies. Major campaigns rarely develop according to the planning scenario. The enemy may appear on the battlefield in greater numbers than anticipated; he may have unexpected fire power in armor and artillery; his antiaircraft defenses may have sufficient depth and integration to disrupt air operations; terrain and weather may both prove treacherous. Careful planning is critical when there will be no one commander-in-chief with a combined staff. The coordination that will be required to integrate the forces in the operation's execution should be anticipated and the coordination agencies established before the campaign begins.

2. Helicopter delivery of troops in a combat assault in a permissive environment is an effective tactic that capitalizes on the advantages of initiative, flexibility and mobility. If possible, the tactical scheme

AIRCRAFT COMBAT LOSSES IN LAM SON 719

NR	AIRCRAFT	CALL SIGN	DATE	UNIT	MISSION	CAUSE	COORDINATES	SPEED	ALT FT AGL	CREW STATUS	SAR
1	F-4D	Cobra 04	11Feb71	12TFW Phu Cat AB	Strike	AW 12.7 mm	N 1641 E 10658		800	1 KIA 1 WIA	YES
2	F-4D	Cobra 33	25Feb71	12TFW Phu Cat AB	Strike	Unk attacking tank	N 1645 E 10628	450	1,500	Recovered	YES
3	F-4D	Gunfighter 44	25Feb71	366TFW Da Nang Afld	Strike	.51 Cal	N 1632 E 10629	400–450	1,000	Pilot-KIA 1 WIA	YES
4	A-1H	SANDY 04	6Mar71	1SOS NKP RTAFB	SAR	Small Arms	N 1640 E 10630	170	50	Recovered	YES
5	A-7	Battlecry 15	13Mar71	Navy	Strike	23 mm	N 1606 E 10632			Missing	YES
6	O-2A	Hammer 244	16Mar71	20TASS Da Nang Afld	FAC	37 mm	N 1648 E 10626		Low Level	Missing	NO
7	F-100D	Blade 82	22Mar71	35TFW Phan Rang AB	Strike	Attacking tank 12.7 mm	N 1638 E 10632	450	Low Level	Missing	NO

FIGURE 17

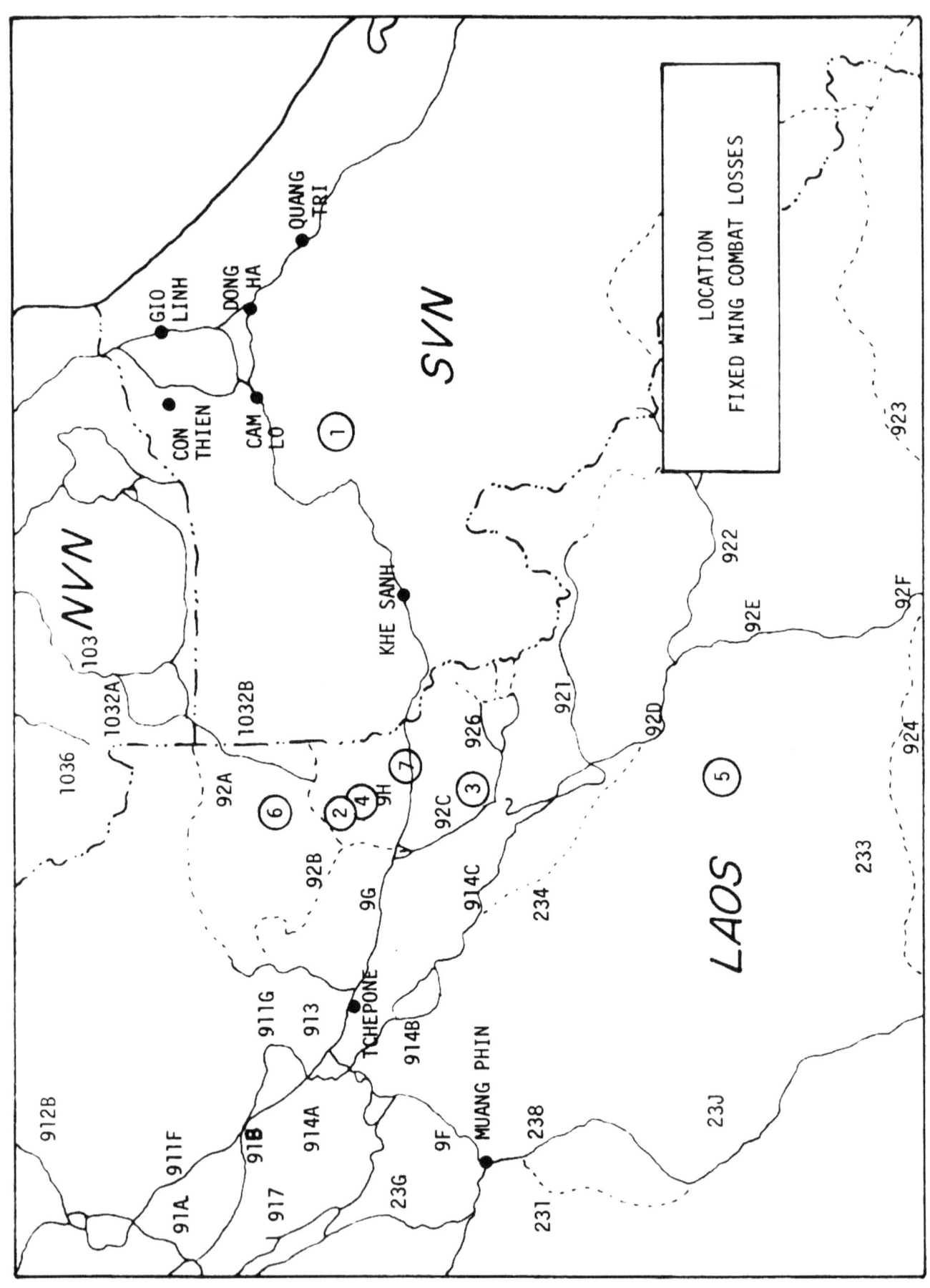

FIGURE 18

of maneuver should be predicated on the exercise of several options in landing sites to permit the assault to be made where enemy resistance is least. For an assault into an area of formidable enemy resistance, it is the task of the Air Force to deliver heavy firepower, integrated with other fires, to suppress the enemy defensive fire so that the assault can be made with minimal risk to the helicopters and troops. Close timing of the landing zone preparation and the combat assault is essential so that the enemy is denied the opportunity to react. To provide a reasonable degree of safety all helicopter operations in a well defended area should be conducted only after tactical air has delivered the necessary suppressive ordnance. Heliborne assaults like airborne assaults are most successful when made into very low threat areas.

3. The selection and preparation of landing zones requires a close, formalized relationship among the on-scene Air Cavalry Commander, the Army Air Mission Commander and the Air Force Forward Air Controller which welds them into a team.

4. The establishment of fixed fire support bases in hostile territory which are dependent upon helicopter resupply and troop extraction without an alternative ground line of communication is not desirable. This ground tactic deprives air of its superior features noted previously and leaves its weaknesses--vulnerability to enemy weapons, limited resources, weather, etc.

5. When the ground forces operate from static positions with limited maneuver, these positions must be so placed that they can provide mutual support between adjacent positions with artillery fire and screening infantry. To rely solely on air-delivered firepower to counter a superior enemy ground force is a poor tactical plan because enemy air defenses, limited air resources, or adverse weather may deny the firepower support at a critical time.

6. While the resources of tactical fighters in Southeast Asia existing during Lam Son 719 insured that some form of air ordnance was always available for close support, such campaigns in the future may not take place in a region where a tactical air force of this size exists. Therefore, to insure the greatest possible responsiveness to the fire support needs of a dynamic ground battle, close coordination of the suppressive fires provided by all services must be maintained.

7. The in-flight coordination procedures between U.S. Army helicopters and tactical aircraft need to be improved. If the airborne forward air controller cannot communicate with the helicopters, a dangerous situation arises--especially within the confines of a small geographic area.

8. Language problems with non-English speaking allies can become critical, particularly in the control of tactical aircraft engaged in close support operations. If interpreters are to be assigned to fly with USAF forward air controllers, it would be highly desirable to establish integrated teams

who could train together sufficiently to work smoothly in the air. Where possible it would be better to use as interpreters USAF officers who are skilled in the ally's language.

9. A tactical fighter with longer loiter time than any presently in the inventory, and with the capacity to carry a wide variety of ordnance, would be especially effective in the close air support role.

10. Laser-guided bombs were perhaps the most efficient weapons to use against enemy gun emplacements and armor.

11. Airlift personnel should be included in the initial planning of all large scale joint operations which will require airlift support. This is necessary so Army planners may understand the capabilities and limitations of airlift and to permit Air Force personnel adequate time to plan and arrange for essential airlift support.

12. Air Force Air Traffic Controllers with Air Force navigational aids and approach facilities should be used in large scale operations such as Lam Son 719 to handle safely the volume of Air Force airlift and Army helicopter traffic at forward operating bases during periods of peak operation. Army GCA equipment is not designed to provide for multiple IFR approaches and departures required during large scale airlift operations. Army Air Traffic Controllers had neither the training nor the experience to control the volume of Army and Air Force traffic at the forward bases in Lam Son 719.

EPILOGUE

Although this report covers the Lam Son 719 operation up to 24 March when the last ARVN units left Laos, the operation continued until 8 April when it was officially declared over. Hammer FACs continued to fly over the area directing air strikes on known or suspected enemy targets, reporting that the antiaircraft fire was more intense than ever. The Commando Hunt V interdiction program continued in the Steel Tiger area of Laos which included Lam Son, and enemy truck traffic within Laos, just after the ARVN troops withdrew, reached a peak for the year, surpassing the truck traffic for a similar period the year before. The ARVN made two fairly ineffectual one-day commando raids into Laos. Activity in Military Regions I and II of South Vietnam stepped up considerably as it did in Military Region IV. The true test of the effectiveness of Lam Son 719, according to many observers, would come in late 1971 and early 1972. The rationale for this view was that Cambodia had bought eight months of security for Military Region III and that the Lao incursion might have the same effect in northern RVN.

SCENARIO

30 Jan 71	D-Day.
31 Jan 71	DASC Victor established at Quang Tri.
4 Feb 71	First C-130 landed at Khe Sanh revealed the runway was too soft and required further preparation.
7 Feb 71	DASC Victor became operational and LZ constructs were executed on four sites. Phase II "Jump Off".
8 Feb 71	The 2d Airborne Battalion occupied Hill 30 at 0325 and the 3d Airborne Battalion occupied Hill 31 at 0809H without enemy contact.
9 Feb 71	First tac air used in support of TIC.
10 Feb 71	1st Armored Brigade reached LZ A Loui.
11 Feb 71	Consolidation Phase began.
12 Feb 71	2/1 ARVN Infantry Battalion Combat assaulted into LZ at FSB Delta.
14 Feb 71	First Combat Sky Spot made in support of Lam Son Operation.
15 Feb 71	Sustained C-130 operations on the MX-19 assault strip at Khe Sanh began.
19 Feb 71	39th Ranger Battalion received the first large-scale enemy attack and perimeter positions were overrun.
20 Feb 71	The 39th Ranger Battalion evacuated their position on the evening of 20 Feb after daily attacks since 18 Feb.
23 Feb 71	4/3 ARVN Infantry Battalion combat assaulted into LZ Brown.

25 Feb 71	FSB 30 and 31 received heavy armor and infantry attacks with FSB 31 overrun. First fixed wing combat loss to automatic weapons fire.
26 Feb 71	Contact continued heavy at FSB 31. ARVN tanks and infantry ordered to join up and move forward to defend FSB 31.
1 Mar 71	Old AM-2 runway opened for C-130 operations at Khe Sanh.
2 Mar 71	Heavy attack by fire on FSB 30. Seventy-nine C-130 sorties flown into Khe Sanh delivering over 916 tons of cargo, 1143 pax and 35,000 gallons of JP-4 - the largest single airlift in a one-day time period during Lam Son 719.
3 Mar 71	Combat assault into LZ Lo Lo from LZ Delta with 42 helicopters hit, seven helicopters lost and 20 nonflyable. Commander of FSB 30 reported 200 casualties, ten friendly APCs and tanks destroyed or damaged, and no food or water for two days. Commander evacuated FSB 30 during the night. Marines were built-up to a full division (three brigades).
4 Mar 71	Fifty-four tac air sorties used to prep LZ Liz for the successful combat assault by the 1/1 and 4/1 ARVN Infantry Battalions.
5 Mar 71	4/2 ARVN Infantry Battalion combat assaulted into LZ Sophia.
6 Mar 71	3/2 ARVN Infantry Battalion combat assaulted into LZ Hope.
7 Mar 71	2/2 ARVN Infantry Battalion established positions around Tchepone (the most western point in the operation).
11 Mar 71	The easterly deployment began.
12 Mar 71	LZ Liz and LZ Sophia abandoned.

13 Mar 71	The 1st ARVN Infantry Regiment encountered heavy contact in the vicinity of LZ Lo Lo reporting 1100 enemy KIA.
15 Mar 71	3/1st ARVN Infantry Battalion evacuated LZ Lo Lo moving to FSB Brown. Operable field artillery was destroyed in place.
16 Mar 71	3d Regimental Command Post and 4/3 ARVN Infantry Battalion lifted from FSB Delta to Khe Sanh.
18 Mar 71	1st Regiment lifted from FSB Brown to Khe Sanh after experiencing heavy contact with enemy since 13 March.
19 Mar 71	The attempt to extract the 4/1 ARVN Infantry Battalion from their position, 19 km east south east of Tchepone, was delayed due to constant heavy enemy fire. During the night of 18-19 March the CO and XO were killed in heavy contact which had reduced effective strength to 180. FSB A Loui evacuated as the Armored Task Force began moving eastward to FSB Alpha.
20 Mar 71	All units experienced contact. The 147th VNMC Brigade reported 1000 KIA (400 KBA) while suffering 85 KIA and 238 WIA.
21 Mar 71	2d Regiment, 1st Airborne Brigade CP and the 5th Airborne Battalion airlifted to Khe Sanh.
22 Mar 71	Armored Task Force stalled south of Route 9 while preparing to cross Xe Pon River. Enemy tanks moving eastward on Route 9 in Laos were stopped before overtaking the friendly column.
23 Mar 71	At 1000H all ARVN Armor and Airborne had crossed into South Vietnam. During the night of 22-23 March FSB Delta was

	overrun and at 1015H tac air destroyed 13 abandoned artillery pieces.
24 Mar 71	Helicopters were attempting to locate stragglers for extraction to South Vietnam. All units were officially listed as withdrawn from Laos.
25 Mar 71	VNMC Recon Teams were inserted into Laos as a rear guard action to stem the enemy's movement into SVN.

APPENDIX A

STATISTICAL APPENDIX

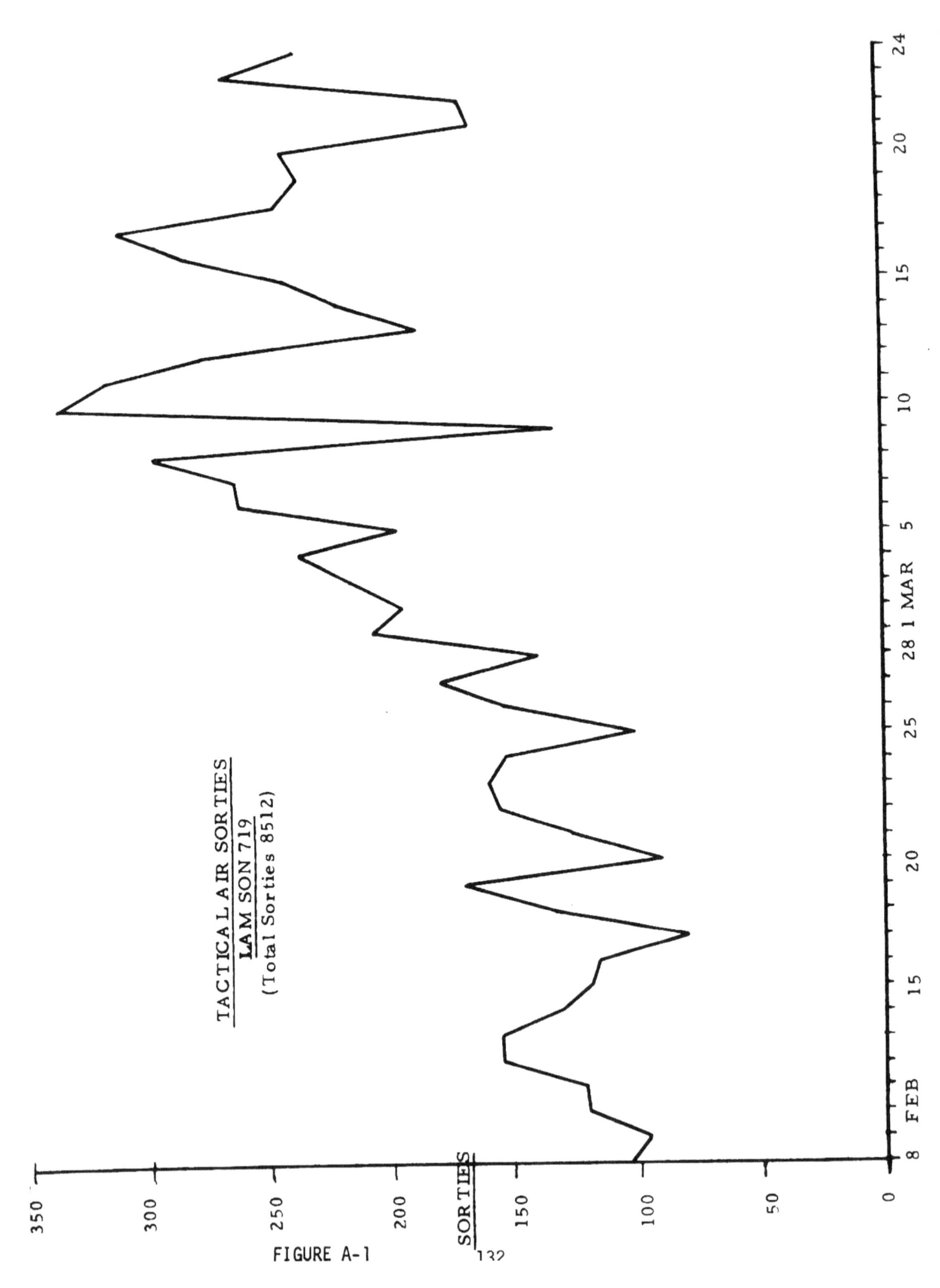

FIGURE A-1

TACTICAL AIR SORTIES IN LAM SON 719

TARGET CATEGORY	SORTIES	PERCENT
PERSONNEL	3593	42.2
VEHICLES *	1433	16.8
DEFENSES **	1284	15.1
LOC INTERDICTION	1111	13.1
STORAGE SITES	538	6.3
OTHER ***	553	6.5

* Includes trucks, armored and auxiliary vehicles and truck parks

**Includes antiaircraft artillery, automatic weapons and weapons positions

***Includes helicopter landing zone construction, fortifications, communication centers, etc.

FIGURE A-2

U.S. TAC AIR DELIVERED ORDNANCE
(SHORT TONS)

LAM SON 719

	EAST		WEST*	TOTAL
3-9 FEB	173.9	8-9 FEB	419.7	593.6
10-16 FEB	264.5		2159.3	2423.8
17-23 FEB	190.3		2162.4	2352.7
24 FEB-2 MAR	248.3		2752.9	3001.2
3-9 MAR	94.7		4213.7	4308.4
10-16 MAR	210.4		4076.6	4287.0
17-23 MAR	214.5		3568.2	3782.7
TOTAL	1396.6		19,352.8	20,749.4

* Lam Son West was that part of the overall AO in Laos

FIGURE A-3

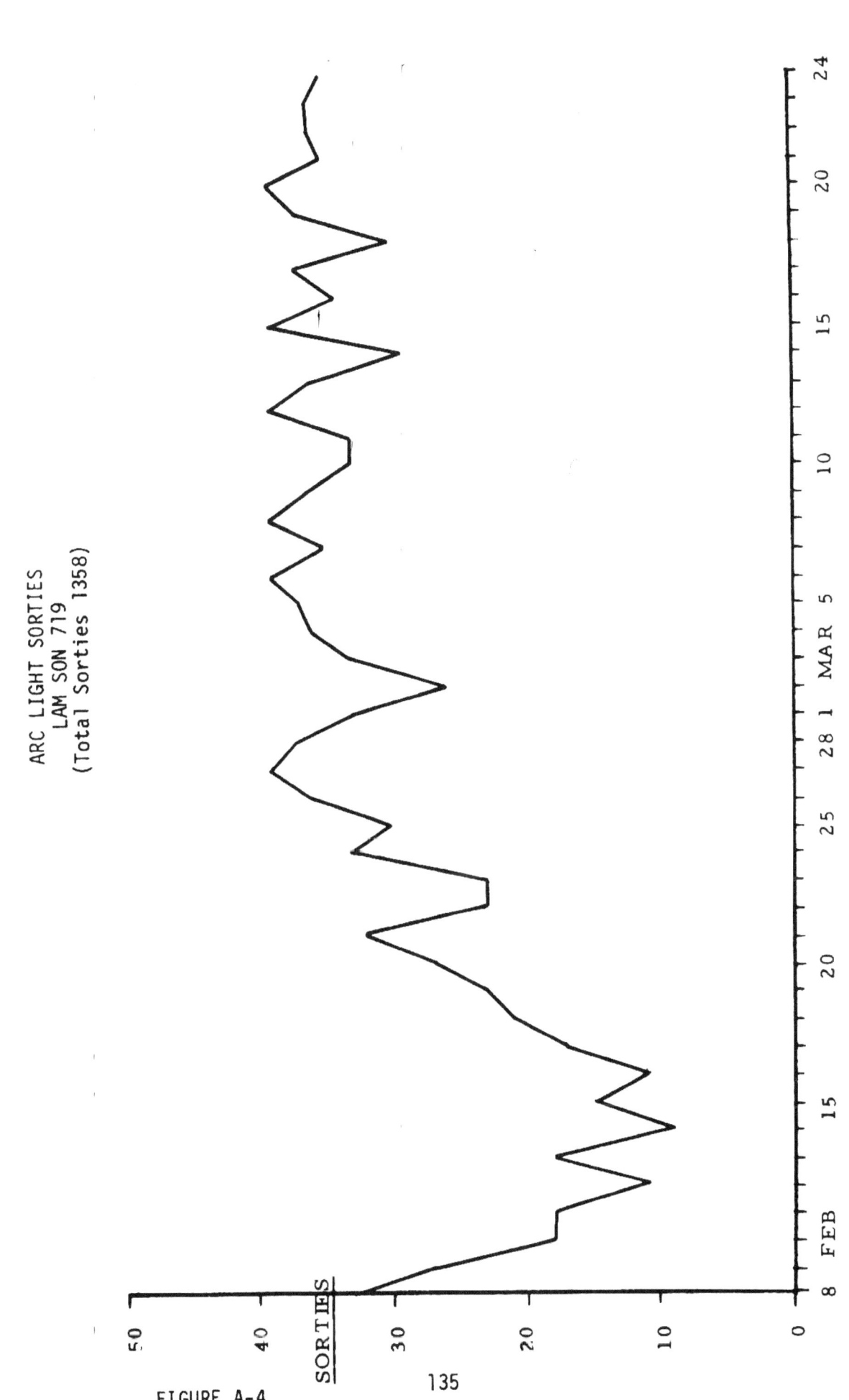

FIGURE A-4

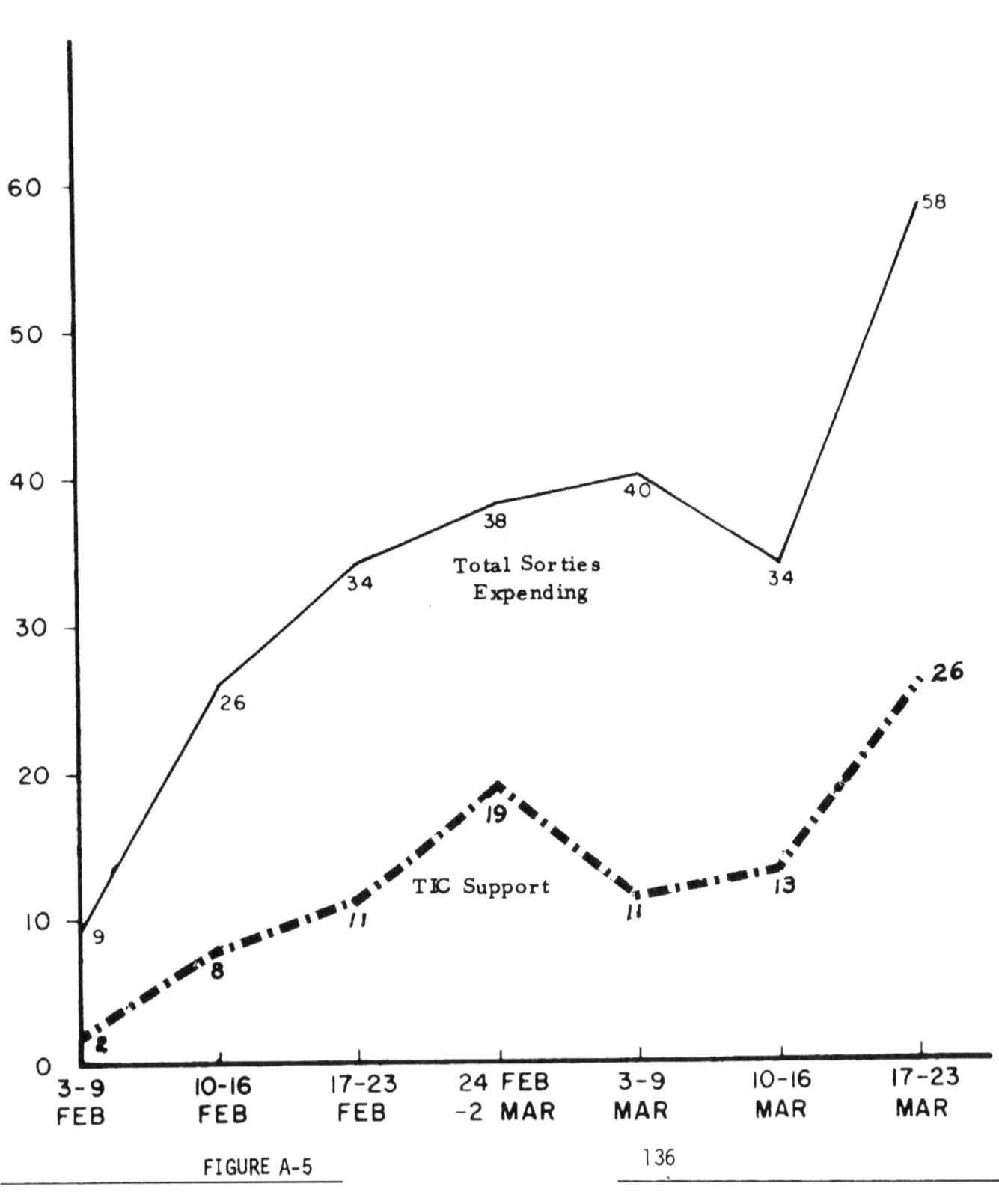

FIGURE A-5

TACTICAL AIRLIFT SUPPORT

LAM SON 719

DATE	MISSION	SORTIES	PASSENGERS	CARGO(S/T)
26 JAN-6 FEB	DEPLOY US SUPPORT FORCES	338	2045	2633.8
30 JAN-6 FEB	DEPLOY CONTINGENCY FORCES	247	9254	1711.5
5 FEB-3 APR	RESUPPLY AND REINFORCEMENT	2083	15545	20513.7
28 MAR-6 APR	REDEPLOYMENT	141	4638	1261.7
	TOTAL	2809	31482	26120.7

FIGURE A-6

BATTLE DAMAGE ASSESSMENT LAM SON 719

REPORTED BY AIRCREWS AND FACS

8 FEB - 24 MAR

TARGET	BDA
PERSONNEL	2307 KBA
FORTIFICATIONS, STRUCTURES	374 DESTROYED 57 DAMAGED
DEFENSES (AA and Automatic Weapons)	225 DESTROYED 48 DAMAGED 54 SILENCED
LOCs	316 CUTS & SLIDES
VEHICLES:	
TRUCKS	1539 DESTROYED 485 DAMAGED
TANKS	74 DESTROYED 24 DAMAGED
OTHER VEHICLES	22 DESTROYED 8 DAMAGED
SECONDARY EXPLOSIONS	9291
SECONDARY FIRES	2049

NOTE: On 24 March, tactical air strikes were also made against abandoned friendly tanks, destroying 14 and damaging 9. These are not reported in the above table.

FIGURE A-7

ENEMY EQUIPMENT CAPTURED/DESTROYED*

THRU 25 MARCH 1971

INDIVIDUAL WEAPONS	4957
CREW SERVED WEAPONS	1913
AMMUNITION	
SMALL ARMS (TONS)	13,631
OTHER (TONS)	479
RICE (TONS)	1550
OTHER FOOD (TONS)	30
MEDICAL SUPPLIES (POUNDS)	7900
RADIOS	96
POL (GALS)	209,710
MISC SUPPLIES AND EQUIPMENT (TONS)	40

*As reported by RVNAF ground commanders

FIGURE A-8

CASUALTIES IN LAM SON 719*

AS OF 24 MAR 1971

	RVNAF	US
KILLED IN ACTION	1118	137
WOUNDED IN ACTION	4081	818
MISSING IN ACTION	209	42

	ENEMY
KILLED IN ACTION	13,341 (KBA 4126)
DETAINED	51

*As reported by RVNAF ground commanders

FIGURE A-9

APPENDIX B

LOGISTICS MOVEMENT APPENDIX

LOGISTICS MOVEMENT

Although the enemy was not forced to shift to western routes, the flow of logistics in Steel Tiger was disrupted by ground action and air strikes in the Lam Son 719 area of operations. That the enemy's logistics flow was disrupted is supported by clear objective evidence, although the longer term effects of Lam Son 719 on the enemy's logistics capability is less clear.

SENSORS MONITORED

The entire sensor field was studied daily, but only selected sensor strings, as shown on the accompanying map are referred to in this analysis of the effects of Lam Son 719 on the enemy's logistics flow. In some instances two or more sensor strings are grouped into a band across parallel route segments for the purposes of studying movement into an area.

NOTE: The term "detection" refers to the activation of one or more sensors in a sensor string. The term "detected movement" refers to the passage of a vehicle past two or more sensors in a strong, for which direction of travel, time and speed could be determined. The detected movements referred to in the text are all presumed to have been truck movements. Truck movements could be differentiated from those of tracked vehicles. Tracked vehicle movements are not included with "detected movements" in this analysis. The information contained in this appendix was taken from an intelligence analysis of Lam Son 719 prepared by 7AF DCS/Intelligence.

TRAFFIC ANALYSIS

South of DMZ:

Sensor strings 09-350 and 09-390 on Route 1032B (Annotation 1 on map)*were used to monitor the input traffic from the DMZ into the eastern Lam Son 719 area. In the five weeks before Operation Lam Son 719 began, movements averaged 12 northbound and 16 southbound each day. Shortly after Lam Son 719 traffic to the south on Route 92B came to a halt as ARVN forces cut this LOC. Nevertheless, traffic detected on the sensor strings along 1032B continued and probably functioned mainly to bring in troops and supplies to counter ARVN forces further south. This traffic fluctuated and generally remained at less than 20 southbound each night although on some nights over 40 southbound movements were detected along this LOC.

Sensor strings 08-480 and 08-540 on Route 92B (Annotation 2 on map) reflected the most dramatic change in traffic patterns caused by Operation Lam Son 719. Previous to 8 February, Route 92B supported roughly the same amount of traffic as Route 1032B as supplies which had entered from the DMZ were moved southward to Route 92C and Base Area 611. The daily average before Lam Son 719 was about 14 movements northbound and 14 southbound, just slightly less than the average on 1032B. There was one surge of activity on 9 February (17 northbound and 32 southbound), then traffic dropped off to zero and remained virtually stopped for the duration of the operation. In summary, traffic on Route 1032B was probably used to support enemy troops in the immediate vicinity, since it did not proceed south to Route 92B.

*Figure B-1 on page 150.

Northeast of Tchepone

Sensor string 09-380 on Route 1035B (Annotation 3 on map) was chosen to monitor traffic moving toward Tchepone and Route 9 from Ban Raving, one of the two input gates from North Vietnam feeding directly into the Lam Son 719 area. The daily average in the five weeks before Lam Son 719 was 14 northbound and 14 southbound movements, increasing weekly from ten to 22 per day. After a short surge of southbound movement on 8-9 February, northbound traffic dropped sharply while southbound movements increased. About 15 March, as the ARVN withdrew from Tchepone, northbound traffic resumed the pre-Lam Son 719 daily average. Southbound traffic continued at a very high level as greatly increased numbers of trucks moved through the Ban Raving entry corridor into Laos destined for the core routes below the Lam Son 719 area. Most of this traffic was not detected along Route 913 moving toward Route 9 and the center of the Lam Son 719 area, rather, it was known to be moving west on Route 9110 to join the main flow onto Route 914 west of Tchepone. Thus, southbound traffic to support troops engaged in the area shifted after the ARVN withdrawal from Tchepone, and became part of the flow through the Tchepone area and southward.

North of Tchepone

String 08-520 monitors traffic moving from the Ban Raving entry corridor to the junction of Routes 913 and 9G, just north of Tchepone (Annotation 4 on map). During four of the five weeks prior to Lam Son 719 an average of nine northbound and 12 southbound movements per day were recorded. In the week immediately preceding 8 February, however, traffic in both directions doubled the previous averages, possibly reflecting the movement of goods out of threatened storage areas. Traffic continued at unusually high levels until 14 February, after which it declined dramatically. Traffic remained very light until the last week in March when vehicles resumed movement along this route.

Northwest of Tchepone

The average daily movements on sensor strings 08-770, 08-820 and 08-840 on Routes 91B, 911G and 918, located northwest of Tchepone, for the five weeks previous to Lam Son 719 was 20 northbound and 18 southbound (Annotation 5 on map). On 8 and 9 February, northbound traffic increased greatly, indicating that the enemy was probably moving stored supplies away from the threatened areas. However, on 10 February, traffic was heavily southbound, almost twice the previous daily average. After one more northbound surge on 13 February, traffic through this area declined and stayed light throughout the remainder of Lam Son 719, averaging four northbound and two southbound movements a day. Thus, after a few surges to move endangered supplies or to support enemy forces, these LOCs served no vital function. The regular logistics traffic that had moved along this route prior to the Lam Son 719 operation was diverted elsewhere.

West of Tchepone

Sensor strings 07-640 and 07-680 monitored the very heavily traveled Route 917, the main route by which traffic from Mu Gia and Ban Karai entry corridors was moved down into Base Area 604 surrounding Tchepone (Annotation 6 on map). Before Lam Son 719, the traffic from these input gates moved either along 91A toward Tchepone or along Route 917 entering the main routes at a point south of Tchepone. But as has been noted, the traffic entering Tchepone from the northwest along 91B, 911G and 918 declined during the Lam Son 719 period. Route 917 was supporting a daily average of 25 northbound and 40 southbound movements before 8 February. During Lam Son 719, Route 917 was generally subjected to heavier use as a high of 60 northbound and 90 southbound movements were detected. Traffic declined throughout Steel Tiger as moon illumination reached a minimum on 23 February. Traffic declined on Route 917 in the last week of March and more traffic appeared to shift to the west on Route 23G. In summary, during Lam Son 719, more trucks from the northern entry gates moved south on Route 917 toward the southern core routes and base areas than in the period prior to 8 February.

Southwestern Lam Son 719 Area

Sensor strings 07-350 and 07-320 monitor traffic on Route 914, the main route network used to move supplies from Base Area 604 to Base Area 611 (Annotation 7 on map). Before Lam Son 719, the daily average of detected movements for the five previous weeks was 24 northbound and 30 southbound. After Lam Son 719 began, northbound movements increased only slightly but there were many days of extremely large increases in southbound movement. Traffic averaged 25 to 40 northbound and over 50 southbound movements each night and on two evenings exceeded 100 southbound movements. After a lull between 24 February and 1 March (detected throughout Steel Tiger), traffic generally leveled off but was still about 40 southbound movers on Route 914 each night. Thus, the very heavy traffic on Route 914 (heavier than that detected on Route 917) reflected the movement of greatly increased amounts of goods southward. These goods probably came from a combination of inputs from Route 917 and Ban Raving, the emptying of threatened storage areas, as well as the localized shuttling of troops and their materiel. There was extensive shuttle activity and many more movements detected on Route 914 than on routes south of 914 leading to Base Area 611. Much of this traffic was, therefore, involved in countering ARVN operations north of Route 914.

South of Lam Son 719 Area

String 10-660 (Annotation 8 on map) monitors traffic entering the Route 99 network, directly south of the Lanong River and reflected the amount of traffic leaving the Lam Son 719 area heading to the major storage areas further south, below Base Area 611. Before Lam Son 719, traffic on this string was erratic but generally averaged 20 north and 20 southbound movements each night. During Lam Son 719, detections increased in both directions, but not to the degree expected if all supplies detected earlier along Route 914B were indeed continuing on to the south.

String 10-610 (Annotation 9 on map) monitors what is basically a secondary Route 929X, leading to the south out of the Lam Son 719 area. Before Lam Son 719 movements on this string rarely averaged more than four northbound and eight southbound each night; movements decreased after 8 February. Most of the increase in traffic which occurred during Lam Son 719 moved south on Route 99 and did not affect Route 929X which is easily interdicted by air strikes.

Throughput to RVN

Sensor string 11-520 monitors traffic going directly toward South Vietnam from Base Area 611 on Route 922 (Annotation 10 on map). Before Lam Son 719 traffic here was steady with a daily average about eight northbound and eight southbound. For the first two weeks of Lam Son 719 the southbound average remained about the same but traffic dropped off to a daily average of less than one northbound and two southbound and with rare exceptions remained at this low level. Southbound movement again increased during the last week of March and supported daily throughput at ten movements.

SUMMARY

The patterns of logistics movement during Lam Son 719 conveyed the enemy's intent to continue using the central route structure. Only once was there any indication of a possible shift to the western Route 23. He abandoned the 1032 and 1035/913 access routes for moving supplies into Base Area 611 and used these routes for direct support to tactical units engaged with the ARVN. The enemy relied on Route 917 and 914 to move goods coming through the entry corridors from North Vietnam and Base Area 604 to points south of the Lam Son 719 area.

These key routes were also used to support enemy tactical forces; since the volume of southbound traffic on Route 914 in the Lam Son 719 area was not reflected further south. However, traffic south of Lam Son 719 area was slightly higher than in the period prior to 8 February. Some of this traffic was almost certainly to move goods away from areas threatened by the ARVN.

Overall, the levels of input from North Vietnam during Lam Son 719 were higher than during the same period in 1970, and after 1 March, the total number of detections throughout Steel Tiger reached a high for this dry season. In part, this may have been necessary to support NVA combat elements in Laos, but mainly the heavy input indicated an enemy intention to continue his logistics effort later in the dry season and perhaps into the wet season. The gradual rise in throughput into South Vietnam and Cambodia, although far below last season's total, continued during Lam Son 719.

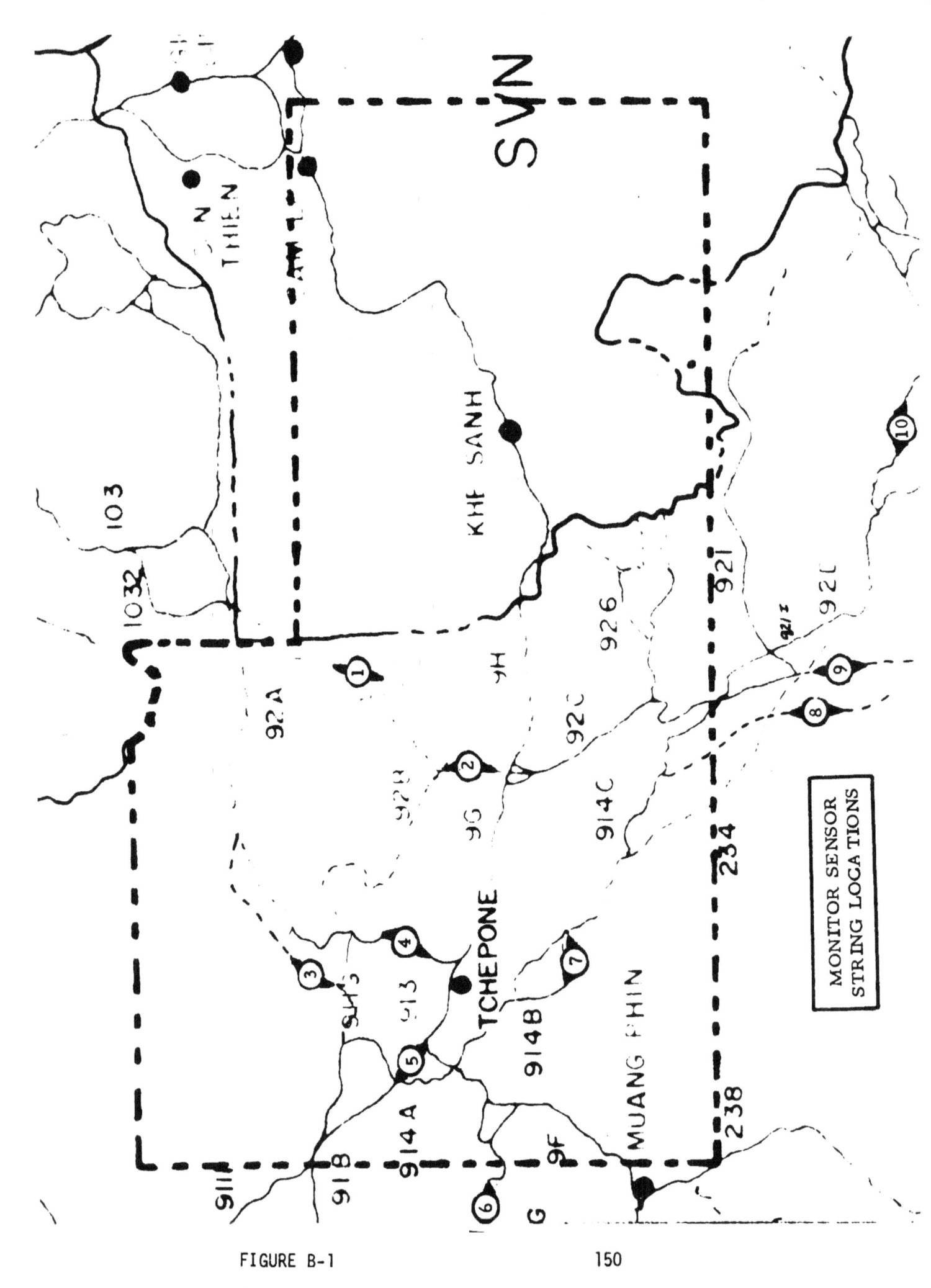

FIGURE B-1

FOOTNOTES*

FOREWORD

1. (U) Report on the War in Vietnam, by Admiral U.S. Grant Sharp and General W. C. Westmoreland (Washington: U.S. Government Printing Office, 30 June 1968)

2. (S) CHECO Report The Battle of Binh Gia, Hq PACAF, 27 Dec 65

3. (TS) CHECO Report Command and Control 1965, Hq PACAF, 15 Dec 66
   (TS) CHECO Report Silver Bayonet, Hq PACAF, 28 Feb 66

4. (S) CHECO Report Operation Birmingham, Hq PACAF, 29 Jun 66

5. (S) CHECO Report Single Manager for Air in SVN, Hq PACAF, 1 Jul 68

6. (S) Lam.Son 719 Intelligence Report #32, Hq 7AF (This recurring report hereinafter cited as 7AF Lam Son Intelligence Report)

CHAPTER I

7. (S) Operations Order, Lam Son 719, Hq XXIV Corps, 23 January 71 (Hereinafter cited as OPORD XXIV Corps)

8. (TS) Msg, General Sutherland to General Abrams, Subj: General Sutherland's Visit to I Corps on 12 Feb 71, 121144Z Feb 71

9. (S) Interview, topic: Operation Lam Son 719, Planning and Initial Execution. With Brigadier General Frederick C. Blesse, Assistant DCS/O, Hq 7AF, by Mr. Ken Sams and Colonel John F. Loye, Jr., at Tan Son Nhut Airfield, RVN, 11 Mar 71 (Hereinafter cited as General Blesse Interview #1)

10. (S) Interview, topic: Operation Lam Son 719 in March 1971. With Brigadier General Frederick C. Blesse, Assistant DCS/O, Hq 7AF, by Mr. Ken Sams and Colonel John F. Loye, Jr., at Tan Son Nhut Airfield, RVN, 7 April 1971 (Hereinafter cited as General Blesse Interview #2)

*Only SECRET information extracted from TOP SECRET references.

11. (S)   G-3 Memorandum dated 24 March 1971 XXIV Corps, Quang Tri, RVN

12. (S)   Mission Summary Data (MISSA), 7AF Intelligence Data Handling System (Hereinafter cited as MISSA Retrieval)

13. (S)   Interview, topic: Operation Lam Son 719. With Major General Joseph G. Wilson, DCS/O, Hq 7AF by Mr. Ken Sams and Colonel John F. Loye, Jr., at Tan Son Nhut Airfield, RVN, 10 March 1971 (Hereinafter cited as General Wilson Interview)

14. (S)   Interview, topic: Operation Lam Son 719, Withdrawal Phase. With Colonel George M. Howell, Director of DASC Victor, by Mr. John Dennison, Quang Tri, RVN, 9 April 1971 (Hereinafter cited as Colonel Howell Interview #3)

15. (S)   Ibid

16. (S)   Ibid

17. (S)   Daily Intelligence Summaries, SACADVON, Hq 7AF, 8 February - 24 March 1971. (Hereinafter cited as SACADVON DISUMS)

18. (S)   MISSA Retrieval

19. (S)   Southeast Asia Data Base (SEADAB) Retrieval, Hq 7AF

20. (S)   Ibid

21. (S)   General Wilson Interview

22. (S(Operations Briefing, Barrell Roll Working Group, Hq 7/13AF, 30 March 1971

23. (FOUO) Memorandum for Record, "Airmobile Operations in Support of Lam Son 719," by Brigadier General Sidney B. Berry, Assistant Division Commander, 101st Airborne Division, 20 March 1971 (Hereinafter cited as General Berry Report)

24. (S)   Lam Son 719, Intelligence Analysis, a working paper prepared by 7AF Intelligence Officers (Hereinafter cited as 7AF Lam Son 719 Intelligence Analysis)

25. (S)   MISSA Retrieval. See also Figure 16 of this report.

26. (S)   General Wilson Interview

CHAPTER II

27. (S)   OPORD XXIV Corps, p B-1

28. (S)   <u>Ibid</u>

29. (S)   <u>Ibid</u>, p B-4

30. (S)   <u>Ibid</u>, p 2

31. (TS)   Operations Order 71-2, Hq 7AF, 28 January 1971, p 4 (Hereinafter cited as OPORD 7AF)

32. (S)   OPORD, XXIV Corps, p 2
    (TS)   OPORD, 7AF, p 4

33. (S)   OPORD, XXIV Corps, p 2 and 3
    (TS)   OPORD, 7AF, p 5

34. (S)   OPORD, XXIV Corps, p 3
    (TS)   OPORD, 7AF, p 5

35. (FOUO)   General Berry Report

36. (S)   General Wilson Interview

37. (S)   General Blesse Interview #1

38. (S)   Operations Order 1-71, I DASC, 28 January 1971, p 2 (Hereinafter cited as OPORD I DASC)

39. (S)   Interview, topic: Operation Lam Son 719, Planning and First 10 Days. With Colonel George M. Howell, Director of DASC Victor, by Mr. John Dennison at Quang Tri, RVN, 18 February 1971 (Hereinafter cited as Colonel Howell Interview #1)
    (S)   Interview, topic: Operation Lam Son 719. With Colonel Aubrey C. Edinburg, DOPF, Hq 7AF, by Colonel John F. Loye, Jr., 21 April 1971 (Hereinafter cited as Colonel Edinburg Interview)

40. (S)   <u>Ibid</u>

41. (S)   OPORD, I DASC, p 1; Appendix 1, p 2; Appendix 2, p 2
    (S)   General Blesse Interview #1
    (S)   Colonel Howell Interview #1
    (S)   Colonel Edinburg Interview

42. (S)   General Blesse Interview #1
    (S)   OPORD I DASC, Appendix 1, p 2

43. (S)   General Blesse Interview #1
    (S)   Interview, topic: Operation Lam Son 719, the Offensive. With Colonel George M. Howell, Director of DASC Victor by Mr. John Dennison at Quang Tri, RVN, 10 March 1971 (Hereinafter cited as Colonel Howell Interview #2)

44. (S)   7AF Lam Son Intelligence Report #19
    (S)   Interview, topic: Operation Lam Son 719. With Major D. J. Creighton, MACV J-2, by Colonel John F. Loye, Jr., 22 Mar 71

CHAPTER III

45. (S)   OPORD XXIV Corps

46. (TS)   Msg, COMUSMACV to Cdr 7AF, Operation Lam Son 719, Report #1 (Hereinafter cited as MACV Lam Son Report #1)

47. (TS)   Ibid

48. (TS)   MACV Lam Son Report #3

49. (TS)   MACV Lam Son Report #4

50. (S)   Description of the airlift operations based on an interview with Colonel Carlton E. Schutt, Deputy Director of Operations for Airlift, 834th Air Division, by Major Gilbert K. St. Clair and Colonel John F. Loye, Jr., at Tan Son Nhut Airfield, RVN, 3 April 1971 (Hereinafter cited as Colonel Schutt Interview)

51. (C)   Command Center Log, Hq Military Assistance Command, Vietnam; 7-8 February 1971, Entry #25 (This Log is hereinafter cited as MACV COC Log)

52. (C)   MACV COC Log for 8-9 February 1971, Entry #41

53. (TS)　　MACV Lam Son Report #11

54. (TS)　　Ibid

55. (TS)　　Ibid

56. (TS)　　Ibid

57. (TS)　　Ibid

58. (TS)　　MACV Lam Son Report #11
    (S)　　 Interview, topic: Ground Operations in Lam Son 719. With Major Alan Winkenhofer, MACV J-306 by Mr. Ken Sams and Major Gilbert K. St. Clair, at Hq MACV, Saigon, RVN, 4 April 1971 (Hereinafter cited as Major Winkenhofer Interview)

59. (TS)　　MACV Lam Son Report #11

60. (TS)　　Ibid

61. (TS)　　MACV Lam Son Report #12

62. (TS)　　MACV Lam Son Report #14

63. (TS)　　Ibid

64. (C)　　 MACV COC Log, 9-10 February 1971, Entry #54

65. (C)　　 Ibid, Entry #55

66. (C)　　 Ibid, Entry #31

67. (TS)　　MACV Lam Son Report #16

68. (TS)　　MACV Lam Son Report #15

69. (TS)　　MACV Lam Son Report #17

70. (TS)　　Ibid

71. (C)　　 MACV COC Log, 11-12 February 1971, Entries #41, 42, 54, 59, and 61

72. (TS)　　MACV Lam Son Report #18

73. (C)　　 MACV COC Log, Item #60, 13-14 February 1971

74. (S)   Daily Intelligence Summary, SACADVON, Hq 7AF, Msg, 140640Z Feb 71 (Hereinafter cited as SACADVON Disum)

75. (S)   Weekly Air Intelligence Summary 71-09, Hq 7AF (Hereinafter cited as 7AF WAIS) p 7-8 and 7AF WAIS 71-10, p 7-8)

76. (S)   7AF WAIS, 71-09, p 7-8 and 7AF WAIS, 71-10, p 7

77. (TS)   MACV Lam Son Report #24

78. (TS)   MACV Lam Son Report #25

79. (S)   Major Winkenhofer Interview

80. (TS)   MACV Lam Son Reports #31 and 34

81. (TS)   MACV Lam Son Report #35

82. (TS)   *Ibid*

83. (TS)   MACV Lam Son Report #37

84. (TS)   MACV Lam Son Reports #37 and 38

85. (TS)   MACV Lam Son Report #40

86. (TS)   MACV Lam Son Reports #41 and 42

87. (S)   Major Winkenhofer Interview

88. (S)   Colonel Schutt Interview

89. (S)   SACADVON Disum Msg, 250235Z February 1971

90. (S)   SACADVON Disum Msg, 220240Z February 1971

91. (S)   SACADVON Disum Msg, 200400Z February 1971

92. (S)   SACADVON Disum Msg, 220240Z February 1971

93. (C)   MACV COC Log, 24-25 February 1971, Entries #60 and 62

94. (C)   MACV COC Log, 26-27 Feb 1971, Entry #62

95. (TS)   MACV Lam Son Report #43

96. (C)   HAMMER FAC Daily Intelligence Summary #54, 23d TASS, Quang Tri, RVN (These recurring reports hereinafter cited as HAMMER FAC Disum)

97. (TS) MACV Lam Son Reports #43 and 44

98. (C) HAMMER FAC Disum #55

99. (TS) MACV Lam Son Report #43

100. (C) HAMMER FAC Disum #56

101. (C) HAMMER FAC Disum #57

102. (TS) MACV Lam Son Report #45

103. (S) SACADVON Disum, Msg, 270227Z February 1971

104. (TS) MACV Lam Son Report #52

105. (C) MACV COC Log, 26-27 February 1971; Entry #62; 27-28 February 1971, Entries #17, 18, 40, 41 and 42

106. (C) MACV COC Log (as corrected), 27-28 February 1971, Entry #52
     (TS) MACV Lam Son Report #50

107. (C) MACV COC Log, 27-28 February 1971, Entry #46

108. (S) Msg, 7ACCS to 7AF, subj: Hillsboro ABCCC Mission Report for Day 28 February 1971, 281301Z February 1971

109. (TS) MACV Lam Son Report #50

110. (TS) MACV Lam Son Report #52

111. (C) MACV COC Log, 28 February-1 March 1971, Entries #27 and 39

112. 9c0 MACV COC Log, 1-2 March 1971, Entry #41

113. (TS) MACV Lam Son Report #54

114. (C) MACV COC Log, 2-3 March 1971, Entry #55

115. (C) MACV COC Log, 2-3 March 1971, Entry #64

116. (TS) MACV Lam Son Report #55

117. (C) MACV COC Log, 4-5 March 1971, Entry #23

118. (C) MACV COC Log, 3-4 March 1971, Entry #61

119. (TS)   MACV Lam Son Report #56
120. (C)   MACV COC Log, 5-6 March 1971, Entry #4
121. (TS)   MACV Lam Son Report #61
122. (TS)   MACV Lam Son Report #64
123. (TS)   MACV Lam Son Report #62
124. (TS)   Ibid
125. (TS)   MACV Lam Son Report #65
126. (TS)   Ibid
127. (TS)   Ibid
128. (C)   MACV COC Log, 10-11 March 1971, Entry #27
129. (C)   MACV COC Log, 9-10 March 1971, Entry #30; 10-11 March 1971, Entry #9
130. (TS)   MACV Lam Son Report #69
131. (TS)   Ibid
132. (S)   SEADAB Retrieval
133. (S)   7AF Lam Son Intelligence Report #014
134. (S)   7AF WAIS 71-12, p 8
135. (TS)   MACV Lam Son Report #71
136. (TS)   MACV Lam Son Report #73
137. (TS)   MACV Lam Son Report #72
138. (TS)   MACV Lam Son Reports #75 and 76
139. (TS)   MACV Lam Son Report #78
140. (TS)   Ibid
141. (TS)   MACV Lam Son Report #79

142. (C)   MACV COC Log, 15-16 March 1971, Entry #56
143. (S)   SACADVON Disum, Msg, 290400Z March 1971
144. (TS)   MACV Lam Son Report #83
145. (TS)   MACV Lam Son Reports #84 and 85
146. (S)   7AF Lam Son Intelligence Reports #19, 20 and 21
147. (TS)   MACV Lam Son Report #84
148. (TS)   MACV Lam Son Report #88
149. (C)   MACV COC Log, 19-20 March 1971, Entries #46, 47 and 48
150. (TS)   MACV Lam Son Report #89
151. (TS)   MACV Lam Son Report #91
152. (TS)   MACV Lam Son Report #89 and 90
153. (TS)   MACV Lam Son Report #87
154. (TS)   MACV Lam Son Report #89
155. (TS)   MACV Lam Son Report #91
156. (TS)   MACV Lam Son Report #90
157. (C)   MACV COC Log, 20-21 March 1971, Entry #53
158. (TS)   MACV Lam Son Report #91
159. (TS)   MACV Lam Son Report #93
160. (C)   HAMMER FAC Disum #155
161. (TS)   MACV Lam Son Reports #95 and 96
162. (TS)   MACV Lam Son Report #93
163. (TS)   MACV Lam Son Report #94
164. (TS)   MACV Lam Son Report #95

165. (TS)   MACV Lam Son Report #97

166. (TS)   MACV Lam Son Report #107

167. (TS)   Ibid

168. (C)   MACV COC Log, 22-23 March 1971, Entries #13 and 38

CHAPTER IV

169. (TS)   Commando Hunt V Report, Hq 7AF, unpublished as of this writing.

170. (S)   Major Winkenhofer Interview

171. (S)   Major General Wilson Interview

172. (TS)   Msg, General Sutherland to General Abrams, Report of General Sutherland's Visit to I Corps on 12 February 1971

173. (S)   Interview, topic: Operation Lam Son 719. With General Lucius D. Clay, Jr., Commander of 7th Air Force, by Colonel John F. Loye, Jr., at Tan Son Nhut Airfield, RVN, 28 April 1971

174. (C)   HAMMER FAC Disum #150

175. (S)   Captain Whitten Interview

176. (S)   Colonel Howell Interview #1

177. (S)   Colonel Howell Interview #2 and Captain Whitten Interview

178. (C)   HAMMER FAC Disum #82

179. (S)   Captain Whitten Interview

180. (FOUO) General Berry Report

181. (S)   7AF Lam Son 719 Intelligence Analysis

182. (S)   Ibid

183. (S)   Ibid

184. (FOUO) General Berry Report

185. (S) General Wilson Interview

186. (S) Ibid

187. (TS) MACV Lam Son Report #50 and 101st Airborne Division (AML) Daily Operations Summary of 28 February 1971

188. (S) General Wilson Interview

189. (C) HAMMER FAC Disum #81

190. (C) HAMMER FAC Disum #82

191. (C) HAMMER FAC Disum #85

192. (C) HAMMER FAC Disum #86

193. (TS) MACV Lam Son Report #58

194. (C) HAMMER FAC Disums #89 and 90

195. (C) MACV COC Log, 5-6 March 1971, Entry #13

196. (TS) MACV Lam Son Report #59

197. (C) HAMMER FAC Disums #93 and 94

198. (C) MACV COC Log, 5-6 March 1971, Entry #31

199. (C) HAMMER FAC Disum #84

200. (S) SEADAB Retrieval

201. (S) Ibid

202. (S) Captain Whitten Interview

203. (S) Colonel Howell Interview #2

204. (C) HAMMER FAC Disum #85

205. (C) HAMMER FAC Disum #69

206. (C) HAMMER FAC Disum #147

207. (S) MISSA Retrieval

208. (S)   General Wilson Interview

209. (S)   Based on data in 7AF Lam Son 719 Intelligence Analysis

210. (S)   Ibid

211. (S)   MISSA Retrieval

212. (C)   HAMMER FAC Disum #147

213. (S)   7AF Lam Son 719 Intelligence Analysis

214. (C)   Combat Vehicle Evaluation, Eurasian Communist Countries, February 1967, U.S. Army Materiel Command

215. (S)   Captain Whitten Interview

216. (S)   MISSA Retrieval

217. (S)   SEADAB and MISSA Retrievals

218. (S)   7AF Lam Son 719 Intelligence Analysis

219. (S)   Working paper prepared by Hq 7AF (INTT)

220. (FOUO) General Berry Report
     (S)   SACADVON Disum, Msg, 290400Z March 1971

221. (S)   SACADVON Disum, Msg, 230400Z March 1971

222. (S)   SACADVON Disum, Msg, 220245Z March 1971

223. (S)   7AF Lam Son 719 Intelligence Analysis

224. (S)   Arc Light BDA Report from MACV J-2, 24 March 1971

225. (C)   Memorandum, Short Rounds Incidents - Lam Son 719, Lieutenant Colonel C. D. Glenn, Hq 7AF (DOCC), to Brigadier General Blesse, 1 April 1971

226. (C)   Ibid

227. (C)   Ibid

GLOSSARY

AA	Antiaircraft
AAA	Antiaircraft artillery
ABCCC	Airborne Battlefield Command and Control Center, AC-130 aircraft equipped with a control capsule
ABN	Airborne
ACS	Armored Cavalry Squadron; Air Cavalry Squadron
AML	Airmobile
AO	Area of Operations
APC	Armed Personnel Carrier
ARA	Aerial Rocket Artillery, helicopters equipped to fire rockets
ARC LIGHT	(S) B-52 strike operations
ARVN	Army of the Republic of Vietnam
AW	Automatic Weapons (12.7 and 14.5mm)
BARKY	Call sign of the Forward Air Controllers (20th TASS) who operated in Military Region I, South Vietnam during Lam Son 719
BARREL ROLL	Northern Laos area of operations for air interdiction and close air support
BDA	Bomb Damage Assessment
BLUE CHIP	7AF Command and Control Center
CHECO	Contemporary Historical Examination of Current Operations
COMBAT SKYSPOT	(S) MSQ-77 controlled bombing
COMMANDO HUNT V	(S) The Northeast Monsoon air interdiction campaign in Southern Laos
COMMANDO VAULT	(S) Employment of the BLU-82 weapon (15,000-pound bomb) with C-130 aircraft to create helicopter landing zones
COMUSMACV	Commander, U.S. Military Assistance Command, Vietnam
CP	Command Post
DAISY CUTTER	(S) MK 82 (500 pound, high explosive bomb) or MK 84 (2,000 pound, high explosive bomb) with fuze extenders designed to explode at the surface of the ground to kill personnel and defoliate
DASC	Direct Air Support Center
DISUM	Daily Intelligence Summary
DMZ	Demilitarized Zone
DTOC	Division Tactical Operations Center
FAC	Forward Air Controller
FSB	Fire Support Base
GCA	Ground Controlled Approach
GIAP	General Vo Nguyen Giap, Minister of Defense of the Democratic Republic of Vietnam (North Vietnam)

G-3	General Staff, Operations
G-4	General Staff, Materiel and Logistics
HAMMER	Call sign assigned to the Forward Air Controllers of the 23d TASS (Augmented) who operated over the Laos portion of the Lam Son 719 Area of Operations
IFR	Instrument Flight Rules
KBA	Killed by Air
KIA	Killed in Action
LGB	Laser Guided Bomb
LOC	Line of Communication
LZ	Landing Zone (Helicopter)
MACV	Military Assistance Command, Vietnam
MAW	Marine Air Wing
NAPE	Napalm, a fire bomb of petroleum jelly
NBL	No Bomb Line
NDP	Night Defensive Position
NVA	North Vietnamese Army
NVN	North Vietnam, North Vietnamese
OFF-SHORE	USAF units permanently located outside of South Vietnam but with elements operating in-country
POL	Petroleum, Oil, and Lubricants
PREP	Preparation, ordnance delivered to suppress enemy weapons fire in the area of a helicopter landing or pick-up
PT-76	Soviet-built, light, amphibious tank
PZ	Pick-up zone (helicopter)
RECON	Reconnaissance
RLAF	Royal Laotian Air Force
RPG	Rocket Propelled Grenade
RVN	Republic of Vietnam (South Vietnam)
RVNAF	Republic of Vietnam Armed Forces
SA	Small arms (7.62mm or smaller)
SAM	Surface-to-Air Missile
SNAKE	Snakeye, MK 82 high drag bombs
STEEL TIGER	(S) Geographic area in Southern Laos designated by 7th Air Force to facilitate planning and operations
TF	Task Force (Armored)
T-34	Soviet-built, medium tank

T-54	Soviet-built, medium tank
Tac Air	Tactical Air, used generally to mean tactical strike aircraft excluding B-52s
TACAN	Tactical Air Navigation System
TACP	Tactical Air Control Party (Post)
TIC	Troops in contact
TOT	Time over target
UHF	Ultra High Frequency
VHF	Very High Frequency
VNAF	South Vietnamese Air Force
VNMC	South Vietnamese Marine Corps

RESEARCH NOTE

The unpublished source materials for this report have been placed on microfilm. The MACV Lam Son 719 report, XXIV Operations Order, Seventh Air Force Operations Order, I DASC Operations Order and the airlift planning documents are all on CHECO Microfilm #TS 94 and TS 97. The Hammer FAC Disums are on CHECO Microfilm #S 438 and S 449. All of the records of DASC Victor are on CHECO Microfilm #S 438, 439, 440 and 449. The interviews, the Seventh Air Force Lam Son 719 Intelligence Analysis, the Memorandum of Brigadier General Berry, USA, and other pertinent analyses are on CHECO Microfilm #S 490.